THE ROYAL FAMILY
QUIZ & FACT BOOK

Previous books by Timothy B. Benford

The World War II Quiz & Fact Book
The World War II Quiz & Fact Book, Volume 2
The Space Program Quiz & Fact Book (with Brian Wilkes)
Hitler's Daughter (A Novel)

THE ROYAL FAMILY QUIZ & FACT BOOK

Timothy B. Benford

PERENNIAL LIBRARY

Harper & Row, Publishers, New York
Cambridge, Philadelphia, San Francisco, Washington
London, Mexico City, São Paulo, Singapore, Sydney

FIRST EDITION

Designer: *Lydia Link*
Layout: *Timothy B. Benford*
Index: *S. W. Cohen and Associates*

Library of Congress Cataloging-in-Publication Data

Benford, Timothy B.
  The royal family quiz & fact book.

  Bibliography: p.
  Includes index.
    1. Elizabeth II, Queen of Great Britain, 1926–   —Family—Miscellanea. 2. Great Britain—Kings and rulers—Miscellanea. 3. Great Britain—Princes and princesses—Miscellanea. 4. Questions and answers. I. Title. II. Title: Royal family quiz and fact book.
DA590.B43   1987   941.085′092′2 [B]   86-46044
ISBN 0-06-096182-1 (pbk.)

87 88 89 90 91 RRD 10 9 8 7 6 5 4 3 2 1

For my paternal grandparents

ARTHUR J. BENFORD, 1882–1965, who served both Her Majesty
Queen Victoria and His Majesty King Edward VII
in the Coldstream Guards

AND

ELLEN BENFORD (née Lynch), 1886–1935, who with her
husband came to America to raise their family

Contents

Introduction

Millions of people from all walks of life, in Britain, throughout the Commonwealth, in the United States, and even in non-English-speaking countries are curious to know about the "royals" and their seemingly fantasy lifestyles.

This obsession with the person royal can be traced back for centuries. King James I (of England) and VI (of Scotland) in the sixteenth century couldn't understand why crowds of people would nearly crush him while trying to get a closer look. "I'll pull down my breeches and they shall also see my arse!" he once offered. Elizabeth, the Queen Mother, puts it more delicately, advising admirers: "Please don't touch the exhibits."

The current members of the royal family, however, experience more media attention than all their predecessors combined, thanks to satellite communications in both the print and broadcast media. People who have never even been on the same continent with any of them can rattle off their birth and wedding dates, favorite foods, and myriad other details one usually only knows about close relatives.

This book brings together hundreds of facts—from the trivial to the fateful, intended to amuse, inform, and surprise you—along with photographs and illustrations of the family, friends, retinue, the foibles, fears, likes, dislikes, and exploits of the royal family.

Perhaps the best comment on the royal family was made by one of their own, King George V, during a visit to St. George's Chapel, Windsor. He stood there amid the remains of all but two of his predecessors since George III and said: "A strange busload to be traveling through eternity together."

Acknowledgments

The most difficult task one faces upon completion of a manuscript is acknowledging all who in one way or another contributed some degree of assistance. The specter of failing to remember someone haunts all authors. At this point I find myself hunting through notes, scraps of paper hastily written, the backs of business cards, old envelopes, and even paper luncheon napkins.

Now the moment of truth. My sincerest thanks and appreciation go to the following for the time, effort, input, suggestions, research, contributions, and support expended on this project:

Daniel Bial of Harper & Row for dreaming up this book and then asking me to do it; Stewart Grainger of the British Information Service;the staff of the Department of Archives, Nassau, Bahamas; Toogood's Photography Studio, Nassau, Bahamas; Captain Alison Ewan, Equerry to H.R.H. The Prince of Wales; Graham Dyer, Curator, the Royal Mint; Judith Frank Kaller, North American agent for the Royal Mint; Jeff Blyth, the BBC and Interpress, London and New York; Louise Collins, WBUX, Bucks County, Pennsylvania; Ralph Howard, WINS, New York; C. Stevens Laise, Federal Hall Memorial Associates, New York; The Archives Department, Trinity Church, New York; Bedford Pace, The British Tourist Authority; Ian Keown, New York; Gregory F. Boyle, Bayonne, New Jersey; James M. Dolan, Jr., Washington, D.C.; Ed and Sandy Hayes, Avenel, New Jersey; Claire and Bill Maher, Mountainside, New Jersey; and Dean Kalousis, Kean College, Union, New Jersey.

THE ROYAL FAMILY
QUIZ & FACT BOOK

Q How many times were Elizabeth II and Prince Philip reported on the verge of divorce during the first twenty-five years of their marriage?

A An average of twice a year, or just over fifty times! The unfounded stories appeared in various British, Continental, and American newspapers. They are seen above in this formal portrait by Karsh of Ottawa in June 1985, some thirty-seven years after their wedding.

—British Information Services

Royal Love Affairs

A marriage begins by joining man and wife
together. But this relationship, however deep,
needs to develop and mature with passing years.
For that it must be held firm in the web of family
relationships, between parents and children,
grandparents and grandchildren, cousins, aunts
and uncles.

—*Queen Elizabeth II*

Q *Who once caused Elizabeth II to run around screaming aboard the Royal Train?*

A Her husband, Prince Philip, wearing plastic vampire teeth and apeing another royal, the Transylvanian Count Dracula. The hijinx occurred when they were still newlyweds, before Elizabeth was Queen.

Q *Which royal Consort was rumored to have been the product of an adulterous affair his mother had with a Jew?*

A German-born Prince Albert, husband of Queen Victoria (1837–1901).

Q *Which member of the royal family renounced his right to the throne in order to marry a divorced Roman Catholic?*

A Prince Michael of Kent, to marry Austrian Baroness Marie-Christine von Reibnitz in 1979.

Q *Name the Prince and future King whose marriage proposals were rejected by no less than six women.*

A William IV (1830–37). Among the ladies who said no were: The Dowager Lady Downshire; Lady Berkeley (daughter of Denmark's King); the Duchess of Oldenburg; and three commoners. William was widely considered "eccentric" in his day.

Take a Seat, My Dear Prince Charles is only one inch taller (71 vs 70) than Princess Diana, and she appears even taller in heels. As a result she is usually seated in formal portraits, as she was in this 1981 photo by Lord Snowdon. If they are on a staircase (as was the case for the engagement portrait), she will be a step below him. In the portrait used for the Commemorative Wedding Stamps, the Prince of Wales was reported to have been standing on a box to create the difference in their height.

—*British Information Services*

Déjà Vu The Prince of Wales once considered marrying Lady Diana Spencer but changed his mind and married Princess Augusta of Saxe-Gotha instead. The Prince in question, however, was Frederick Louis, son of George II (1727–60), and father of George III (1760–1820). He died in 1751, nine years before his father's reign ended and, therefore, his son rose to the throne that had eluded him. Additionally, the *first* husband of Wallis Warfield Spencer Simpson, the future Duchess of Windsor, was Earl Spencer. Princess Diana's father is also Earl Spencer.

Q *Which royal sent aides to evaluate the oral hygiene of the woman he was arranging to marry?*

A Henry VII (1485–1509), whose intended wife was the Queen of Naples, a widow and the daughter of Edward IV (1461–70). He also wanted to know the size of her breasts.

Q *Name the King who used a bright candle to physically examine the intended bride of his son, the Prince of Wales.*

A George I (1714–27), who wanted to be sure Princess Caroline of Brandenburg-Anspach was worthy of the future George II (1727–60).

Q *Which twentieth-century royal's name was linked with models, actresses, dancers, and a beauty queen before he was married?*

A Prince Andrew, who like his grand-uncle Edward VIII (1936) and great-great-grandfather Edward VII (1901–10), gained a reputation as a Prince with an eye for the ladies.

Q *Identify the monarch who reportedly slept with Winston Churchill's mother, Jennie Jerome Churchill.*

A Edward VII (1901–10), while he was still Prince of Wales. Also reportedly included among his many conquests were British actresses Lillie Langtry and Margot Tennant.

The Nuptial Numbers Game Much is made of the fact that Henry VIII had six wives, but little is said about his last wife, Catherine Parr, who was married four times: twice before Henry and once after he died. The last man she married, Thomas Seymour, had also been married four times. Even Henry's first wife, Catherine of Aragon, had been married previously (to Henry's late brother, Arthur).

Q Which Queen reportedly carried on at least two intimate relationships with other women?

A Queen Anne (1702–14), first with her childhood friend, Sarah Jennings (later the wife of John Churchill, the first Duke of Marlborough); in her later years Sarah was replaced by Abigail Masham. Anne's husband and Consort was Prince George of Denmark, with whom she had five children.

—*British Information Services*

The Price of Love   When Princess Margaret and Group Captain Peter Townsend were considering marriage, she discovered that to marry a divorced man she would have to remove herself from the line of succession and forfeit her annual state allowance. These conditions were proffered by her sister, the Queen, who had desperately sought some compromise to the outright prohibition of the marriage favored by the Prime Minister and others in the government. Margaret and Peter determined that without her state allowance their love would have a difficult time surviving on his Royal Air Force pay.

Q *What do the following women have in common: Lady Jane Wellesley; Lady Sarah Spencer; Jane Ward; Sabrina Guinness; and Anna Wallace?*

A At one time or another they were romantically connected to Prince Charles by the press.

Q *Which royal once expressed the biting opinion that she hoped Prince Charles wouldn't marry a divorced American?*

A The woman who knew better than anyone else the problems such a matching could create, the Duchess of Windsor.

Q *Name the former girlfriend of Prince Charles who was featured in a naked photo spread in* Penthouse *magazine.*

A Fiona Watson.

Q *Identify the twentieth-century royal who was presented with a naked woman on a silver platter when he requested a delectable dish at a Paris restaurant.*

A Edward, Prince of Wales (future Edward VII), in 1875 at the Café des Anglais.

Q *Name the heart-throb of Prince Andrew who starred in the porn flick* Emily.

A Kathleen Norris; stage name, Koo Stark.

By Appointment   If your mother or mother-in-law is Queen of England, you just can't drop in for lunch or a before-dinner drink. As cold as it may seem, the children and daughters-in-law of Elizabeth II must make an appointment, via the Queen's private secretary.

Sealed with a Kiss   When Prince Charles responded to the cries of the crowd below the balcony of Buckingham Palace and kissed his new bride, Diana, he did something that had never previously been done in the history of the House of Windsor. However, five years later his brother Prince Andrew and his new bride, Sarah, established the "Balcony Kiss" as a Royal Wedding tradition as they played the crowd and did likewise.

—*British Information Services*

> **Love and Marriage**   Perhaps one of the loveliest stories about Queen Victoria and Prince Albert has to do with a royal family feud. So distraught was the Prince after a heated domestic quarrel that he withdrew to the private quarters and locked himself in. Victoria marched up to the door and knocked on it strongly. "Who's there?" queried Albert. "The Queen of England," she stated firmly. There was no reply. Victoria knocked again, this time louder. Again the question: "Who's there?" and her reply, "The Queen of England!" Albert continued to ignore her. This went on for a few more times, with Victoria knocking harder and raising her voice with each question from Albert. Finally a much softer knock came. Albert again intoned, "Who's there?" but this time the voice was also softer, "Your wife Victoria, Albert." He opened the door at once.

Q *Who owned the villa on the Caribbean island of Mustique that Prince Andrew took Koo Stark to after he returned from action in the Falklands war?*

A Princess Margaret, his aunt. It was while they were there that the Queen and Prince Philip first learned that the young lady they had entertained at Balmoral and whom they realized their son was quite serious about had appeared in a sex film. They voiced their concerns to him via telephone calls. The trip, and love affair, ended abruptly.

Q *Which modern-day Prince abided by his bride's wish not to consummate their marriage on the wedding night?*

A Prince Michael of Kent, first cousin of Elizabeth II, who married Austrian Baroness Marie-Christine von Reibnitz in 1979. As a Catholic, she thought she had to abstain from sex to remain in a state of grace and receive Holy Communion the next morning.

Q *Name the royal who got so drunk on his wedding night he passed out before consummating the marriage.*

A George, Prince of Wales (future George IV, 1820–30), on April 8, 1795. He was reportedly still in love with his first wife, a Roman Catholic whom he married secretly ten years earlier.

> **Young Lovers**   Mary, Princess Royal, daughter of Charles I (1625–49), was nine years old when she married William of Orange in 1641. Her husband was fourteen. She gave birth to William III of England (1689–1702) ten years later. She was the last of the child brides.

Q Who officiated at the marriage of Edward, Duke of Windsor, and the twice-divorced Wallis Simpson?

A Reverend Robert Anderson Jardine, an Anglican clergyman who defied the Church of England's ban on marrying divorced people. Seen in photo above on their wedding day in 1937, they had gone through a civil ceremony shortly before the religious one.

—British Information Services

> **Preference Surfaced Early**   Even before he gave up his throne for the woman he loved, the American divorcée Wallis Simpson, Edward had earned a reputation for becoming romantically involved almost exclusively with married women. From 1915 until 1918, he was romantically connected to Lady Coke, a woman reportedly twelve years older than the Prince. He then had relationships with Mrs. Dudley Ward (for sixteen years) and Lady Furness. These only ended when he became serious about Wallis Simpson.

Q *Name the cleric who officiated at the wedding of Prince Andrew and Sarah Ferguson on July 23, 1986.*

A The Archbishop of Canterbury, Robert Runcie, who also united Prince Charles and Diana.

Q *How long did it take for Sarah Ferguson to walk up the aisle of Westminster Abbey on her wedding day?*

A During rehearsals for her wedding to Prince Andrew, the march had been precisely timed at three and a half minutes. On the eve of the wedding, however, her father was quoted as saying: "I don't doubt I will be told by Sarah not to walk too fast or walk faster . . . " Three and a half minutes it was.

Q *How long did Edward VIII's reign as King last in 1936?*

A For only 325 days before he abdicated on December 11, 1936, to marry the "woman I love." He and Wallis Simpson were married in France on June 3, 1937.

Q *Prior to Princess Margaret's divorce from the Earl of Snowdon, when was the last divorce in the royal family?*

A Not since Henry VIII (1509–47) cut his ties to Catherine of Aragon, and the Catholic Church.

> **Amused . . . At First**   Ernest Simpson, the American shipping magnate who was the second husband of Wallis Warfield, was at first amused as he watched a close relationship develop between his wife and the Prince of Wales in the early 1930s. That feeling turned to concern as the years passed and, eventually, to indifference. He attended their wedding in 1937 and remained in contact with the couple until his death in 1958.

Princess Anne Oakley   Although she is better known for her equestrian talents, Princess Anne also has a keen eye for shooting. She
scored eleven bull's-eyes from a burst of twenty submachine rounds
at a British Army base in West Germany some years back. She and
husband Captain Mark Phillips were captured in this Norman Parkinson portrait in 1982.

—*British Information Services*

Fact No member of the royal family may marry without permission of the reigning sovereign, according to a 1772 law created by George III (1760–1820). The King was distressed over marriages of two of his brothers, one to a woman said to be illegitimate and the other to a widow. Violators risk losing their civil rights, property, and personal belongings. Also, the marriage could be declared null, leaving any children from such a union as bastards.

Q *Which member of the present royal family admitted to having a hangover the day after Prince Charles and Lady Diana's wedding?*

A Princess Anne, during a public appearance at the Royal Navy base in Portland. She asked her audience's pardon for her slow speech, explaining why.

Q *Identify the modern-day Princess who reportedly locked her husband out of their bedroom after he had drunk too much.*

A Princess Anne, during a visit to Hamburg, West Germany, in 1976. They disagreed over his drinking and charges that he had ignored her at a party that evening.

Q *Which of the women Prince Charles dated came closest to becoming his wife?*

A The general feeling is that Anna Wallace came within a breath of being proposed to had not her feisty temper eliminated her. Charles had been seeing her regularly for nearly a year and several Buckingham Palace regulars were convinced she would be the future Princess of Wales. However, in August 1980, during a party celebrating the eightieth birthday of the Queen Mother, Anna's pride was offended when Charles apparently spent more time with other people in the room. She took him to task for this clearly within earshot of several guests. It was her last appearance with him in public. Eleven months later he married Diana.

Q *How did Princess Margaret meet her future husband, Tony Armstrong-Jones?*

A She was a guest at a wedding he had been hired to photograph.

Dessert Fit for a Queen The popular creamy pudding-based dessert Charlotte Russe was named after the wife of George III (1760–1820), Queen Consort Charlotte Sophia.

Q Which coronation employed coaches rented from a movie studio to dress it up?

A Elizabeth II's. No less than six coaches had previously been sold to a film studio during an economy binge under George VI. When time came for his daughter to be crowned, it was discovered that there were not enough available to create the regal mood. There was no shortage of coaches or other amenities to create the mood regal when Prince Andrew and Sarah Ferguson were married on July 23, 1986.

—British Information Services

Q How large were the crowds that filled the streets of London for the wedding of Prince Charles and Lady Diana in 1981?

A One million people were estimated to have cheered the royal couple on. However, the worldwide television audience was reported to be 750 million. They are seen on their wedding day going through Trafalgar Square in the glass coach—then seventy-one years old—that five years later would also carry Prince Andrew and Sarah Ferguson on their wedding day.

—British Information Services

Q Name the young woman Prince Charles became so serious about that he asked the Queen Mother to instruct her on royal protocol and life as Princess of Wales.

A Lady Jane Wellesley, daughter of the current Duke of Wellington, who decided life in a fish bowl just wasn't for her. The Queen Mother Elizabeth is seen above in this 1950 portrait.

—*British Information Services*

An Act of Love   Elizabeth, the Queen Mother, has kept the desk used by George VI at the weekend retreat, Royal Lodge, exactly as it was when he last used it. It exists today in that state, replete with family photographs, inkwell, clock, and other items.

Q *Who designed the wedding dress worn by Princess Anne for her 1973 wedding to Captain Mark Phillips?*

A Maureen Baker. Medieval in inspiration, it was of white silk satin and had seed pearls outlining the high neck, bodice, and sleeves.

Q *For whom did David and Elizabeth Emanuel design a royal wedding dress?*

A Lady Diana Spencer, for her marriage to Charles, Prince of Wales, in July 1981. It was a crinolined ball gown style in silk taffeta with huge puffed sleeves, lace ruffles, and bows. They gave her the dress as a gift and received many times its actual value in the publicity the dress and the act generated.

Q *Who designed the gown Sarah Ferguson wore the day she married Prince Andrew and became the Duchess of York?*

A Lindka Cierach, the daughter of a Polish war hero, who first entered the fashion world through a secretarial job at the London College of Fashion. After a stint working with leading designer Yuki, she began her own business and operated out of one room of her shared apartment. She also designed the dresses worn by Sarah's four bridesmaids.

Q *Identify the young lady whose past love life caused an end to her promising relationship with Prince Charles.*

A Davina Sheffield. The sensational tabloid press in Britain was quick to pick up that Charles's interest in her was more than just a passing fancy and, always looking for headlines, uncovered gossip that questioned her chastity. True or not, such suspicions do not go hand in hand with the selection of a potential Queen Consort.

Old Flames Die Hard   Shortly after Prince Charles and Lady Diana were engaged, he attended a luncheon of the Scottish Council at which the chairman mistakenly toasted "Prince Charles and Lady Jane!" Jane Wellesley was one of the women Charles was reported to have been in love with prior to Diana.

Love, Honor and Obey   When Sarah Ferguson became the bride of Prince Andrew on July 23, 1986, she reverted to vows first set forth in 1662 and last used by Queen Elizabeth II when she married Prince Philip on November 20, 1947. They include the promise to "love, honor and obey." Princess Diana, however, uttered the alternate marriage rite (of 1928) which omits the word "obey."

—*British Information Services*

> **Largest Gift**   Prince Andrew and Sarah Ferguson received upwards of 10,000 wedding gifts for their July 1986 marriage, but the largest single one was $1 million from Andrew's mother, Queen Elizabeth II.

Q *Name the two items Sarah, Duchess of York, listed among things she and Prince Andrew needed but had not received as wedding gifts.*

A A set of silver and a "fridge" (refrigerator). She noted to all who might be interested that both were available "from Harrods," the famous department store.

Q *How old was Queen Victoria's eldest daughter, Vicky, when Frederick III of Prussia proposed to her?*

A Fourteen, and he was twenty-three. They were married three years later, in 1858. Their first child, the future Kaiser Wilhelm II of Germany, was born in 1859.

Q *Who made the 5'6", five-decker wedding cake for Prince Andrew and Sarah Ferguson's wedding?*

A The Royal Navy. The cake was transported some 250 miles by road from the naval school to London.

Q *Who were the only two attendants at the wedding of Princess Anne and Captain Mark Phillips?*

A Prince Edward, her youngest brother, and Lady Sarah Armstrong-Jones, her cousin.

Q *Was the engagement of Prince Charles and Lady Diana officially announced immediately?*

A No. The announcement came on February 24, 1981. Diana had accepted Charles's proposal earlier in the year, but he had suggested she think it over for a month to consider whether "it was going to be too awful" living in the public eye.

> **Protocol**   When Prince Andrew and Sarah Ferguson married, protocol dictated that only wedding gifts from those who had received official wedding invitations could be accepted.

The Palace Pearl Caper?   Princess Elizabeth wanted very much to wear the double strand of pearls (seen above) her parents had given her for her November 20, 1947, marriage to Prince Philip. However, they were on display at Kensington Palace with other gifts the couple had received. An aide was dispatched to retrieve them but had a difficult time explaining this to suspicious detectives. When he returned, he was under the "protection" of three policemen.

—British Information Services

Sleeping on the Job   The ends to which designers will go to protect a Royal Wedding dress from being copied, photographed, or simply seen in advance of the wedding day seem to have no bounds. When Sir Norman Hartnell created the dress worn by Princess Elizabeth for her 1947 marriage to Philip, he not only had the windows of his establishment whitewashed to prevent snooping but he also slept on the premises as the work progressed.

Q *How did Princess Anne and her future husband, Mark Phillips, meet?*

A He had been invited to a dinner party in order to round out the guests to an even number of people.

Q *How did the future Princess Diana meet her future husband, Prince Charles?*

A He was dating her sister Sarah and walking on the grounds of her family estate when they came across each other. She was sixteen, he was twenty-nine, at the time.

Q *How much did the engagement ring cost that Prince Charles gave Lady Diana?*

A At the prevailing exchange rate at the time its estimated value was $42,500.

Q *When did Sarah Ferguson meet her future husband, Prince Andrew?*

A They had known each other from early childhood since the Ferguson family were frequent guests of the royals. One report says their first encounter was at "a high-spirited children's tea party."

Extra Coupons Needed   Even though the marriage of Princess Elizabeth and Prince Philip on November 20, 1947, took place more than two full years after the end of World War II, clothing was still rationed in Britain. As a result the future Queen had to be provided with extra coupons to obtain Lullingstone silk and other material needed for her wedding gown and accessories. The move was a positive step in raising morale for a country still having a difficult time with postwar shortages. The gown has been described as the grandest of the century, and featured a fitted bodice with a long fluted skirt in heavy white silk satin. Its main feature was the embroidery of five-petaled flowers, roses, ferns, and seed pearls of various shapes.

Q What special piece of furniture did Prince Charles have installed aboard the royal yacht *Britannia* in advance of his honeymoon?

A A double bed. The traditional sleeping accommodations aboard are single beds. When Charles's sister Princess Anne and her husband Captain Mark Phillips used the *Britannia* for part of their honeymoon, they had simply pushed two single beds together to be cozy.

—*British Information Services*

She Didn't Love Him Anymore   Don't read this if gory things bother you: Edward II (1307–27) holds the distinction of perhaps suffering the most repulsive if not painful death of any British monarch. His Queen Consort Isabella, with her lover Roger Mortimer, disposed of Edward in favor of his son Edward III. After having him kept in prison for nine months she apparently decided it was time to rid herself of the former King. He was held down, a funnel forcefully inserted in his rectum, and a red-hot pointed shaft rammed through it into his bowels.

Q *Which royal publicly denied any romantic involvement several times in the months prior to the official engagement announcement?*

A Princess Anne, who said such reports about her and Captain Mark Phillips were just rumors.

Q *How many times did Buckingham Palace deny that any engagement between Princess Elizabeth and Prince Philip had or would soon take place?*

A No less than a dozen times, five of which were "official."

Q *Identify the Queen Consort who was married to two successive kings.*

A Matilda, first wife of Henry I (1100–35), and only wife of his nephew and heir, Stephen (1135–54).

Q *Who is considered to have been the first commoner to kiss the hand of Diana, Princess of Wales?*

A A student at Dean Close School named Nicholas Hardy, who had half-jokingly asked if he might kiss the hand of his future Queen. In an impish mood, she obliged.

Q *In total, how many people went aboard the royal yacht* Britannia *with newlyweds Prince Charles and Princess Diana?*

A Counting the officers, aides, crew, and musicians, Charles and Diana were all alone at sea with 311 people. Besides Diana there was only one other woman aboard, her maid!

At Least None Became Old Maids   No less than seventeen foreign Princesses, most between ten and fifteen years old, came to England prior to the year 1500 to become Queen Consorts.

Q Name the British lord who the press speculated would marry The
Queen Mother after the death of George VI (1936–52).

A Sir Arthur Penn, a longtime friend and associate of both her and
the late King. The Queen Mother is seen above with the Duke and
Duchess of Kent attending the Royal Variety Performance at the
Prince of Wales Theater, London, in November 1961.

—British Information Services

The Wedding That Wasn't   Until he ascended to the throne, George V and his wife Mary of Teck were troubled for years by a rumor that he had married a woman in Malta in 1890. According to one version, when his brother Albert, the Prince of Wales, died in 1892 and George became second in line to the throne (behind his father the future Edward VII), the reigning Queen Victoria instructed that the marriage by nullified and George marry Mary of Teck, the woman who had been engaged to his late brother. After a successful 1910 libel trial against a French newspaper which had published an unsubstantiated account, the rumor all but ceased to circulate.

Q *Which royal was mistaken for a housemaid by a Coldstream Guard who then proceeded to flirt with her?*

A Queen Victoria in 1889. She had opened a second-floor window at Windsor Castle on a warm summer evening and it attracted the attention of a nearby guard who came over and began a conversation. She retreated quickly despite calls of protest from the lonely guard. He never knew to whom he had suggested such romantic sentiments.

Q *Which Prince claimed his boat broke down in explaining why he returned home very late after a date?*

A Prince Philip in Venice, Italy, in 1938. He said the boat experienced spark plug problems.

Q *Name the mistress who took rings and other jewelry off the body of a dying monarch.*

A Alice Perers, mistress of Edward III (1327–77). However, she is credited with having earlier given him something: the gonorrhea that caused his death.

Q *Who was best man at the wedding of Princess Anne and Captain Mark Phillips?*

A Captain Eric Grounds.

Understanding Wife   Edward VII's romantic involvement with Mrs. Alice Keppel was common knowledge. His wife, Queen Alexandra, displayed what must be the ultimate degree of tolerance when she sent for Mrs. Keppel and personally escorted her to the King's deathbed. Alexandra was once quoted as saying: "A royal mistress should curtsey first . . . and then jump into bed."

Q Who did George VI ask in 1946–47 to look into the background of Prince Philip in an effort to determine whether Philip was worthy of the hand of Princess Elizabeth?

A The task fell to RAF Group Captain Peter Townsend, who himself would be deemed unworthy of Elizabeth's sister, Princess Margaret, some years later. "What infernal cheek," Philip commented, "for a man who was already heading for divorce to set himself up as a marriage counsellor!" Princess Elizabeth and Lieutenant Philip Mountbatten are seen above at Buckingham Palace in the first post-engagement photo of the couple in 1947.

—British Information Services

First Impressions Princesses Elizabeth and Margaret first met Prince Philip of Greece when they accompanied their father, George VI, on an inspection of Dartmouth Naval College in 1939. The two Princesses were impressed with how high he could jump and how much food he could eat. Elizabeth was thirteen and Philip eighteen at the time. Eight years later they would marry.

Q *Identify the head of state whose request to be invited to the 1973 wedding of Princess Anne and Captain Mark Phillips was ignored.*

A Idi Amin of Uganda.

Q *Name the song Prince Charles requested to be sung at his wedding to Princess Diana.*

A "I Vow to Thee, My Country."

Q *At which Royal Wedding was "O Perfect Love" requested by the loving couple?*

A The marriage of the Duke of Windsor and Wallis Warfield Simpson.

Q *Which royal requested that the jaunty American tune "A Bicycle Built for Two" be played at his wedding?*

A George, Prince of Wales (future George V).

Q *Name the King who had monuments built at all the places his wife's coffin stopped on its return to England.*

A Edward I (1272–1307), son of Henry III (1216–72). His wife, Queen Eleanor, was the daughter of Ferdinand III of Castile and Leon, Spain. They were married in 1254 and she died in 1290 while traveling with him during the Crusades. According to one version, she sucked poison from a battle wound which otherwise would have killed him; it did kill her.

Unlucky Child Bride, Twice Princess Joan, daughter of Edward III (1327–77), was sent to Austria at age four to become the bride of the Duke. She was returned to England a year later when the English King and Austrian Duke failed to solidify their alliance. At age fourteen she was sent to Spain to become the bride of Prince Pedro, but she died of the plague before the marriage could take place.

"Kiss Me, Kiss Me, the camera is watching!" was just the kind of spontaneous and candid statement that made Sarah Ferguson such a delight with royal-watchers. Fergie uttered the impish words to Prince Andrew during a nationally broadcast British television interview the night before the couple took their vows at Westminster Abbey on July 23, 1986. The Prince obliged and playfully retorted: "You're a monster." Photo above was made available to the press some weeks before the wedding.

—*British Information Services*

One-Hour Photo Service   In the crunch to publish news and photos of the Royal Wedding of Prince Andrew and Sarah Ferguson, some publications went to extremes, employing helicopters, race car drivers, and all sorts of state-of-the-art electronic transmittal systems. One of the more elaborate schemes was employed by the American supermarket tabloid, *The Star.* Color transparencies were beamed via satellite 22,000 miles above earth to a printing plant in Hackensack, N.J. Each photo took less than one minute to transmit. Total elapsed time from taking the photos at Westminster Abbey, developing them, and transmitting them to the United States was less than an hour.

Q *Which future Queen Consort changed her first name after marriage to a Prince of Wales?*

A May of Teck, who became Mary when she married the future George V (1910–36).

Q *Which married royals are second cousins via relationship to King Christian IX of Denmark?*

A Elizabeth II and Prince Philip, who are also third cousins by virtue of Queen Victoria.

Q *Name the married royals who are seventh cousins via the Duke of Devonshire.*

A Prince Charles and Princess Diana, who are cousins no less than nine other ways through common relatives and ancestors.

Q *Identify the married royals who are thirteenth cousins in two separate ways.*

A Princess Anne and Mark Phillips. One of their relationships is via Edward I.

Wishful Thinking?   The adversarial relationship between George IV (1820–30) and various Founding Fathers of the former British Colonies which became the United States was only surpassed by the King's dislike of Napoleon Bonaparte of France. So it was quite natural that upon learning of the death of Bonaparte in the second year of George IV's reign, Frederick, Duke of York, should announce: "Your greatest enemy is dead!" The King, who was at odds with his wife, Queen Caroline, responded: "By God, is she?" The Queen died later that year.

Q When he was Prince Philip of Greece, where did the future husband of Queen Elizabeth II stand in line for his country's throne?

A He was fifth in line for the Greek throne, an eighteen-month-old infant, when his family had to flee the revolution in 1922. He is seen above accompanying his wife, Elizabeth II, to the installation ceremony of the Knights of the Garter at St. George's Chapel, Windsor, in 1957, the year she made him a Prince again.

—*British Information Services*

Randy Command Performance   While still sowing his wild oats prior to marrying Sarah Ferguson, Prince Andrew caused a bit of tisk-tisking on both sides of the Atlantic by attending a bump-and-grind striptease joint in Florida. Palace hopes that the incident would blow over in a few days were shattered when worldwide news services reported that the owner of the club had posted a new sign outside renaming the act "The Randy Andy Eye Popper."

Q *Which of Henry VIII's (1509–47) marriages lasted the longest and the shortest?*

A The longest was his first, to Catherine of Aragon, twenty-three years. The shortest was to wife number four, Anne of Cleves, six months.

Q *How many of Henry VIII's six wives outlived him?*

A Only two: his fourth wife, Anne of Cleves, who died ten years after him, and his last wife, Catherine Parr, who died one year after him.

Q *Identify the King who was forty years older than his Queen Consort.*

A Edward I, Longshanks (1272–1307), who married Princess Margaret, daughter of Philip III of France, after the death of his first wife, Princess Eleanor, daughter of Ferdinand III of Castile and Leon.

Q *Name the King who was eleven years younger than his Queen Consort.*

A Henry II (1154–89), who married Eleanor, Duchess of Aquitaine, the former wife of Louis VII of France. However, he was older than his mistress, Rosamond Clifford.

Q *Name two future Queen Consorts who were first engaged to older brothers of the men they eventually married.*

A Mary of Teck, who was first engaged to Albert, Prince of Wales. After he died, she married his younger brother, the future George V. Earlier, Catherine of Aragon had been married to Arthur, Prince of Wales, and upon his death she married his younger brother, the future Henry VIII.

Q *At which Royal Wedding did the orchestra begin tuning their instruments in an effort to let the sermonizing Archbishop know he had spoken long enough?*

A The marriage of the Prince of Wales (future Edward VII) and Princess Alexandra, daughter of Christian IX of Denmark.

From Mulberry Leaves to Royal Silk   Silkworms at Lady Hart Dyke's silk farm in London Colney, Hertfordshire, were treated to extra portions of their staple diet, mulberry leaves, to help them produce the high-quality silk ordered for the cot cover and pillow slips for Princess Margaret's first child in 1961. The farm building was once used by Nell Gwynne and is named after her. Lady Hart Dyke's worms have also provided silk for coronations and royal weddings.

—*British Information Services*

> **Well, It Couldn't Hurt** Convinced that royalty could influence trends in dress, manners, etc., twenty-one-year-old Queen Victoria ordered that Honiton lace be used as much as possible for her wedding on February 10, 1840, to Prince Albert. As a result, the lace industry in England overcame a difficult economic period.

Q *Which royal turned down the first two proposals of marriage from the man she eventually married?*

A The Queen Mother, who didn't expect the future George VI (1936–52) to be so persistent and ask a third time.

Q *Why did Charles and Diana choose St. Paul's Cathedral over the traditional Westminster Abbey for their wedding?*

A The acoustics were considered a major factor. Their wedding included a solo by opera soprano Kiri Te Kanawa, two full choirs, and three orchestras.

Q *How large was the guest list to Prince Charles and Lady Diana's wedding?*

A A reported 2,321 invitations were sent out. Of this number the groom's family issued 2,100+, while the remaining 200 or so were for use of the bride's family.

Q *Had Lady Diana's father footed the bill for her wedding to Prince Charles, what would it have cost him?*

A At the exchange rate of the day it came in at just over $250,000. Elizabeth II and Prince Charles himself reportedly contributed $150,000 of the cost and the rest came from the government . . . which easily recouped its expenses through the selling of worldwide television rights.

Q *Thanks to television, which Royal Wedding to date has been witnessed by the largest audience?*

A That of Prince Charles and Lady Diana in July 1981, which, experts say, was tuned in by 750 million people.

Q *Which Princess raised eyebrows when she handed a flower to a young sailor who presented a bouquet to her during ceremonies to launch a Royal Navy ship?*

A Princess Margaret, in 1947. It was the same year in which she met Group Captain Peter Townsend for the first time.

Q Identify the London firm charged with decorating the top tier of Prince Charles's christening cake.

A The top tier of Elizabeth and Philip's wedding cake was redecorated by McVitie & Price and used as the top tier of the christening cake. The cake itself was made by students of the National Bakery School.

—*British Information Services*

Catholics Need Not Apply   The 1701 Act of Succession provides that no one in the line of succession to the throne can marry a Roman Catholic. The Queen at that time, Mary II, was the daughter of a Catholic.

Q *Name the King who, as a Prince, divorced his wife of twelve years on the grounds of infidelity and had her imprisoned for life.*

A George I (1714–27), while he was still a Prince in Germany. His wife, and cousin, Sophia Dorothea of Celle, spent thirty-two years imprisoned, and died a year before him.

Q *Identify the two Queens who were crowned on their wedding days.*

A Matilda of Scotland, on November 11, 1100, first Consort of Henry I (1100–35), the youngest son of William the Conqueror; and Berengaria of Navarre, daughter of King Sancho VI, who became the bride of Richard I (1189–99), Coeur de Lion, on May 12, 1191.

Q *Name the Scots King and Queen Consort who had a private Roman Catholic coronation prior to their public one.*

A James II (1437–60) of the House of Stewart and his wife, Mary of Guelders. Their reign in Scotland took place during that of Henry VI of England (1422–61).

Q *Name the yacht that Edward VIII and Wallis Simpson cruised on during their eastern Mediterranean summer vacation in 1936.*

A The *Nahlin.*

Q *Which item of dress, from her wedding sixty-one years earlier, was buried with Queen Victoria?*

A Her wedding veil, which covered her face.

Q *Where did Sarah, Duchess of York, continue working after her marriage to Prince Andrew?*

A As London director of BCK Graphics, an art publishing house, where she earned approximately $25,000 per year.

Q *Who was the only reigning monarch to marry a reigning monarch of another country?*

A Mary I (1553–58), known as Bloody Mary. She married King Philip II of Spain.

Q What was the maiden name of Queen Elizabeth, the Queen Mother?
A Elizabeth Bowes-Lyon, seen above in 1907 at age seven.

—*British Information Services*

Royal Children

Here's to the Queen and Albert gay
And all the children too, hurray
May another come the first of May
For another royal christening.
—*Victorian Ballad*

Q *Which Prince once dumped bubblebath soap into the Windsor Castle fountain?*

A Teen-aged Prince Andrew, as a prank. He was following in the footsteps of his father Prince Philip, who at age five turned several pigs loose that ran amok during a party.

Q *Which Prince once used a top hat to throw up in?*

A Though Henry VIII (1509–47), if top hats existed then, or Edward VII (1901–10) would have been good guesses, it was neither. Prince Philip did it at age fifteen when he became extremely sick during a visit to Greece.

Q *Which Prince put a whoopee cushion on a bishop's chair?*

A Prince Charles, who put it on the seat of a chair being used by the Bishop of Norwich while the churchman was visiting Sandringham.

Q *Name the oldest Queen Consort to give birth.*

A Queen Eleanor, wife of Edward I (1272–1307), known as Longshanks because of his long legs. She was forty-six years old when her fifteenth child was born. Three, including the last, died in infancy. (When Eleanor died in 1290, Edward married Princess Margaret, the daughter of King Philip III of France, who gave him three more children. He also fathered at least one bastard son, John Botetourt.)

Fact Royal titles are handed down through the male members of the family (exception is the immediate family of the monarch). As a result, Princess Margaret's children, Viscount Linley and Lady Sarah, got their titles because their father is titled, not because their mother is the Queen's sister. Peter and Zara, the children of the Queen's daughter, Princess Anne, and Mark Phillips, seen above, do not have titles because their father is not titled.

—*British Information Services*

The Royal Two-Step?   When Princess Anne discovered as a child that Buckingham Palace sentries had to present arms each time she passed them, she delighted in going back and forth and watching them snap to several times.

Q *Which King and Queen had the most children?*

A The undisputed champions at royal parenthood are George III (1760–1820) and Queen Charlotte, who had fifteen children. Theirs was said to be a happy marriage, more than can be said of his relationship with the American Colonies.

Q *Name the first royal, in direct line of succession to the throne, to be born in a hospital.*

A Prince William, the first son of Prince Charles and Diana. Diana herself had been born in her mother's bed, while Charles was born in a large bathroom at Buckingham Palace that had been equipped to serve as a delivery room.

Q *Who was the oldest Queen Consort to give birth to a future sovereign?*

A Queen Eleanor, the second wife of Henry II (1154–89) and former Duchess of Aquitaine (she had previously been the wife of Louis VII of France). She was forty-five years old when she gave birth to the future King John (1199–1216). However, John did not reign immediately after his father but followed Richard I (Coeur de Lion, 1189–99), to the throne.

Q *Identify the Prince of Wales whose wearing of a sailor suit caused a children's fashion boom.*

A Prince Albert Edward, second child of Queen Victoria and Prince Albert. The suit began a trend that continued for more than fifty years. It may have been revived in 1986 when four-year-old Prince William, son of the current Prince of Wales, wore a sailor's suit as an attendant at his uncle Andrew and new aunt Sarah's wedding.

Fact   Prince Andrew once hid beneath a table in the dining room at Buckingham Palace and proceeded to reach up and remove the knives and forks as quickly as they were being placed down by servants.

Trend Setter at Age Three   The future Elizabeth II, seen at age three in this 1929 photo, was on the cover of *Time* magazine that year wearing a yellow dress. Predictably, yellow became the "in" color in fashion for some time afterwards. The photo above was taken at Glamis Castle, Scotland.

—*British Information Services*

Sales Snowballed When Prince William was photographed in a snowsuit displaying the initials "ABC" in January 1984, there was an immediate and insatiable demand for the garment. Stocks of the snowsuit sold out within twenty-four hours of the photo's publication. Meanwhile, intrepid manufacturers who had large quantities of regular snowsuits made an immediate killing by having "ABC" patches attached.

—British Information Services

Q Name the four royal cousins all born in 1964.

A In the order of their birth they are: James Ogilvy, Princess Alexandra's first son; Prince Edward, youngest child of Queen Elizabeth II; Lady Helen Windsor, daughter of the Duke of Kent; and Sarah Armstrong-Jones, daughter of Princess Margaret. James Ogilvy is seen above with his sister Marina and their parents Princess Alexandra and Angus in the garden of their home at Thatched House Lodge, Richmond Park, in 1970.

—*British Information Services*

He Should Have Sold Tickets James II (1437–60), the Catholic sovereign of Protestant England, invited no less than sixty people to witness his second wife giving birth. He did this to prevent his enemies from making future claims that the child was not heir to the throne. His precedent-setting efforts went for naught, however, since it was soon rumored that the infant had been introduced to the birth bed hidden in a warming pan and in fact was not his. His enemies prevailed and James, and his son, lost the throne. (The tradition of having witnesses present continued up to and including the births of Princess Elizabeth and Margaret. It wasn't abolished until their father became George VI.)

Q *Who was the last child crowned King?*

A James VI of Scotland, who at one year old when he was crowned in 1567, was also the youngest.

Q *Who holds the distinction of being the first royal baby born in Scotland since Charles I (1625–49)?*

A Princess Margaret Rose, sister of Queen Elizabeth II, who was born at Glamis Castle, owned by her maternal grandfather the Earl of Strathmore, on August 21, 1930.

Q *Who was the first member of the royal family to win a scholarship?*

A George, Earl of St. Andrews, born in 1962, eldest of the Duke of Kent's children, who won a prestigious King's Scholarship to Eton.

Q *Who was the first member of the royal family to be sent to school with other students?*

A Prince Edward (future Edward VIII), who was sent to Osborne Naval College in 1909. The step was considered a startling break with tradition. However, his father, George V, wanted him exposed to the general public.

Q *What were Prince Charles's favorite subjects in school?*

A He was partial to history, geography, and painting. Like his mother, mathematics were barely tolerated.

Parental Instincts Queen Victoria had been an only child, while her husband Albert had one brother. However, they were the parents of nine children: five daughters and four sons.

Let the Breezes Blow　　The kilts worn by the royals include extra weight in them so they won't rise in a strong breeze or wind and thereby provide photographers with an unusual photo opportunity. The Duke of Edinburgh and Prince Charles were caught in this "like-father-like-son" pose wearing the Balmoral Tartan at the Braemar Gathering in Scotland in September 1955.

—British Information Services

I'm Glad You Liked It, Dad   As a young man, Edward, Prince of Wales, convinced his father George V to take time from the royal schedule and sit back while Edward played the bagpipes. Despite much practice Edward had a difficult time mastering the wind instrument. The King listened in disbelief, not recognizing a single tune Edward proudly announced. Finally the king rose, held up his hand, and told his son: "Don't do this again. My advice is leave this art to the Highlanders, they know what they're doing!"

Q *Which King fathered the most children?*

A Henry I (1100–1135), the Lion of Justice, who is credited with twenty-four children: three by his two wives, Matilda and Adelicia, and twenty-one with two mistresses, Nesta of Dehuebarth (South Wales) and Elizabeth de Belloment, his favorite.

Q *Identify the royal who as an adult slept in baby-type sleeper pajamas that totally covered his feet.*

A Prince Albert, husband of Queen Victoria (1837–1901).

Q *Where was Elizabeth II born?*

A At 17 Bruton Street, London, the home of her maternal grandparents, with whom her parents were staying while looking for a home of their own in London. She was the first monarch born in a non-royal home.

Q *When was Elizabeth II born?*

A On April 21, 1926. However, her birthday is celebrated by her subjects on a variable day in June, usually the second Saturday. The tradition originated with Queen Victoria, who wanted to spend the anniversary of her birth each year with her family and close friends. Thus, a second date was selected for the day-long public displays.

Q *Name the only King born after his father died.*

A William III (1689–1702), who was born on November 14, 1650, nine days after the death of his father, Prince William of Orange. He followed his maternal uncle, James II (1685–88), to the throne.

They Made Grandma Happy   Seven of Queen Victoria's grandchildren grew up to become: an Emperor (Germany); Empress (Russia); and five Queens (Greece, Norway, Rumania, Spain, and Sweden).

In Her Majesty's Service   Just like Bond, James Bond's, a custom-made Aston Martin was given to Andrew, Prince Andrew, for his sixth birthday. The miniature car had a price tag of £4,000 and came replete with toy machine guns that popped out, a "smoke" screen, and other typical Bond goodies. However, for his fourth birthday older brother Prince Charles had to make do with a pedal car. In birthday photo above, he is equally amused by a glove puppet.

—British Information Services

Q Which Princess was given a speeding ticket for fast driving?

A Princess Anne, who has been stopped for fast driving more than once, and at least once was issued a speeding ticket. She is seen above practicing in 1959 at the wheel of a bumper car during a circus visit.

—British Information Services

Charles III and William V   could very well be the two monarchs who follow Elizabeth II to the throne—provided her son and grandson continue in the line of succession and elect to keep their own names. The last monarchs of those names were: Charles II (1660–85), who like Prince Charles was also Prince of Wales and Duke of Cornwall; and William IV (1830–37), who had been Duke of Clarence. In the 1984 photo above, Princess Diana holds young Prince Henry, while Prince William is with Prince Charles.

—British Information Services

Family Ties   Henry VIII's son, Edward VI (1547–53), became King at age nine upon the death of his infamous father. Always in poor health, he ruled only six years before he also died. However his uncle, the Duke of Northumberland, convinced the young sovereign to leave the crown to the King's sixteen-year-old cousin Lady Jane Grey, rather than to his Catholic half-sister Mary, the legitimate heir. Lady Jane, who was Queen for only nine days, also happened to be married to the Duke's son. Older and cunning Mary (remember Henry VIII was also *her* father) easily took control and had Jane executed within the year.

Q *How old was Prince Charles when he was sent to Cheam boarding school?*

A Eight years old. It was the same school his father, Prince Philip, had attended.

Q *Name the outpost of Geelong School that Prince Charles attended in Australia for two terms.*

A Timbertop. Charles described it later as "the most wonderful experience I've ever had."

Q *What college did Prince Charles attend?*

A Trinity College, Cambridge, with an interruption for a term at Aberystwyth University to learn Welsh before his investiture as Prince of Wales.

Q *Which future monarch, as a child, was spanked by a repairman for disturbing his tools?*

A Elizabeth II, who continued to disturb the tools after a repairman installing telephone wires had repeatedly asked her to abstain. His tap on the fanny caused her to run to the future Queen Mother (at the time in 1931 still the Duchess of York), who told her she should not have been doing that.

Tough Job   Barnaby Fitzpatrick never had a tutor or regimented education of any kind. However, he was whipped frequently for insufficient preparation of schoolwork. According to a diary kept by Edward VI (1547–53), Master Fitzpatrick was punished whenever the King didn't know his work. Fitzpatrick was the whipping boy.

Grandfathers On the day he died, the ailing King George VI had felt well enough to go on a shooting expedition with Lord Fermoy. Twenty-nine years later George VI's grandson, Charles, would marry Lord Fermoy's granddaughter, Lady Diana. The King and Prince Charles are seen together at Buckingham Palace in this 1952 photo.

—*British Information Services*

Musical Debut Lord Nicholas Windsor, son of the Duke of Kent, set a royal precedent in 1980 when he was ten years old by appearing at Covent Garden in Mozart's *Magic Flute.*

Q *Who were "the Princes in the Tower"?*

A The uncrowned Edward V (1483) and his brother Richard, twelve and ten years old, respectively, when their father, Edward IV (1461–83), died. Their uncle, Richard of Gloucester, had them declared bastards and imprisoned in the Tower of London. He then became King. (See Appendix: The Kings and Queens Since 829.)

Q *Which one of Henry VIII's six wives gave him the son he so desperately wanted?*

A After divorcing his first wife and executing his second, it was wife #3, Jane Seymour, who produced the desired heir, Edward VI (1547–53). She died shortly after childbirth.

Q *Name the son of Mary, Queen of Scots, who was crowned King of Scotland at one year old in 1567 and upon the death of Elizabeth I in 1603 became King of England.*

A James VI of Scotland, who became James I of England. He became King of Scotland when his mother lost the support of her lords, abdicated in his favor, and fled to England, never to see her son again.

Q *Who is the oldest of Elizabeth II's royal cousins?*

A Prince Richard, Duke of Gloucester.

Q *Identify the cousin of James VI of Scotland who was thought to be the sovereign's homosexual lover.*

A Esme Stuart, who arrived from France when James was thirteen years old. He was reported to be the first person to show the young King any friendship or affection. Rivals for the King's favor at Court, however, resented him, and James was forced to send Esme away hardly two years after their initial meeting. James later married Anne of Denmark, with whom he had several children.

Fact Princess Victoria, eldest child of Queen Victoria, was born in 1840 and died the same year as her mother, 1901.

Q Which of Queen Elizabeth II's children was the first born to a reigning British sovereign in more than 100 years?

A Her third, Prince Andrew. Both Prince Charles and Princess Anne
were born before Elizabeth II was Queen. Prior to Andrew's birth
in 1960 the last child born to a reigning British sovereign was Princess Beatrice, youngest child of Queen Victoria, on April 14, 1857.
Queen Elizabeth II and her daughter Princess Anne are seen here
at Frogmore Lake at Windsor in November 1959 before the pregnancy was publicly announced.

—British Information Services

Buckingham "Hospital"   All four of Elizabeth II's children were born at Buckingham Palace.

Q *Identify the first King of England to be born there.*

A Henry III (1216–72), Duke of Aquitaine, the second husband of Eleanor of Provence.

Q *Name the first King born to parents who were both English.*

A Henry IV of Bolingbroke (1399–1413).

Q *Who gave Prince Andrew a wooden rocking elephant for his second birthday?*

A His eldest brother, Prince Charles, who had made it in his school's woodshop.

Q *Which royal once passed out exploding cigars as a joke?*

A Prince Charles, who gave them out to friends after dinner one evening at Dartmouth.

Q *Who was the only King of England to father three future English sovereigns?*

A Henry VIII (1509–47). They were, in order: Edward VI (1547–53); Mary I (1553–58); and Elizabeth I (1558–1603). (The Scots King Malcom III [1058–93] fathered four monarchs, who did not reign in sequence: Duncan II [1094]; Edgar [1097–1107]; Alexander I [1107–24]; and David I [1124–53].)

Q *Where was Prince Charles christened?*

A Because the chapel at Buckingham Palace had not been restored from the bombing it received during World War II, Prince Charles, the thirty-ninth in descent from Alfred the Great, was christened in the Music Room. He wore the same Honiton lace robe that had been worn by the children of Queen Victoria.

Increasing the Empire?   Perhaps because she was so young and of prime childbearing age when she became Queen, Elizabeth II was the subject of no less than ninety-six incorrect reports of being pregnant between 1952 and 1968.

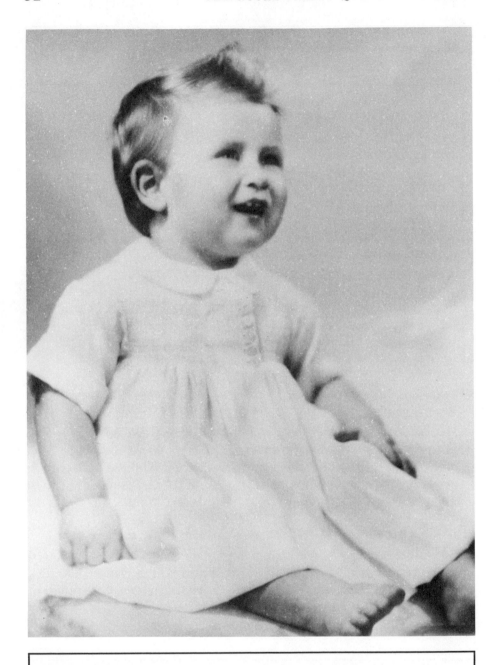

Keeping a Prince Dry When Prince Charles was born in 1948, his mother, the future Elizabeth II, received nearly 1.5 tons of diapers as gifts from people in the United States. He is seen above on his first birthday.

—*Marcus Adams photo*

Q When was Prince William of Wales born?

A The son of Prince Charles and Princess Diana was born on June 21, 1982. He and his father are seen together on his second birthday.

—British Information Services

Q Identify the first member of the royal family to go to boarding
school.

A Princess Alexandra, daughter of Prince George, Duke of Kent, and
a first cousin of Queen Elizabeth II. Her father was the youngest
surviving child of King George V and Queen Mary. Princess Alexandra is seen above in 1966 with her second child, Marina.

—British Information Services

Wrap It Up . . . Like Everybody Else   In 1947, George VI and his family toured South Africa in an effort to show the people of Britain and the Commonwealth that things had returned to normal after the war. At one stop the Queen Mother, wearing a flowery, sumptuous hat, was reportedly the center of attention when a Zulu warrior broke through the security line and rapidly advanced on the royal party. Instinctively she began pounding him with her umbrella . . . until she realized all he was trying to do was give Princess Elizabeth some money as a twenty-first birthday present.

Q *Name the doctor who delivered Elizabeth II's first grandchild.*

A Dr. George Pinker, Surgeon Gynecologist to the Queen, delivered a 7-pound, 9-ounce boy, Peter, to the Queen's daughter Princess Anne and her husband Mark Phillips on November 15, 1977.

Q *Who are the godparents of Prince Charles and Princess Diana's firstborn son, Prince William Arthur Philip Louis of Wales?*

A King Constantine of Greece; Lord Romsey; Princess Alexandria; the Duchess of Westminster; Lady Susan Hussey; and Laurens van der Post.

Q *Identify the sovereign who discontinued the ceremony of having debutantes presented at Court.*

A Elizabeth II, who in 1958 ended the tradition which had begun with Queen Anne (1702–14).

Q *Which royal was rumored to be mentally retarded at birth?*

A Prince Andrew, born in 1960. He was one of a long list of royal children whose births over the years have provided grist for the rumor mill. Usually such unfounded gossip runs rampant until the baby is seen by the press and public.

Sickly Offspring   The intermarriage of royals to each other over the years produced a closeness in bloodlines that frequently resulted in poor health: Prince John, youngest son of George V, was a severe epileptic who died at age thirteen; Prince Leopold, youngest son of Queen Victoria, was a hemophiliac who didn't reach his thirty-second birthday; Prince Albert, eldest son of Edward VII, and as such heir to the throne, was sick throughout his life and died of pneumonia at age twenty-eight.

She Who Laughs Last   Three of the four children of Lord Spencer all have members of the royal family as godparents. The exception is Diana. But her husband and firstborn son, Prince William, are both in direct line of succession to be King. Diana hoists William a bit higher to satisfy requests of photographers in this 1982 photo.

—British Information Services

Fact When it was officially announced that Princess Diana was pregnant the second time, a farmer tried to give Prince Charles a pig's bladder as a gift, insisting the organ would ensure the birth of twins. Charles refused the assistance.

Q *Which Queen was incorrectly rumored to be pregnant when she was fifty-two years old?*

A The Queen Mother, Elizabeth, shortly after the death of George VI in 1952. Some royal-watchers actually debated that if a male were born after Elizabeth II had risen to the throne, a constitutional crisis would exist: would Elizabeth have been declared Regent? Could she be forced to abdicate for a male heir?

Q *Which member of the royal family wrote a best-selling children's book?*

A Prince Charles was the author of *The Old Man of Lochnagor* some years ago. It was originally intended as a gift for his two younger brothers.

Q Black Beauty *was the favorite childhood reading of which royal?*

A Elizabeth II. As she grew older, her equestrian reading expanded to include myriad books, fiction and nonfiction, about horses.

Q *Which future King won a prize for imitating a donkey?*

A George VI, in 1912, when he was seventeen years old, at an equestrian field meet in which riders had to imitate another animal while putting their horses through the course.

Q *Name the royal who won a cake-eating prize as a child.*

A Prince Philip, who was seven years old when he consumed more muffins than any other competitor in a 1928 Paris event.

From the Mouths of Babies As a young child, Princess Elizabeth and her grandfather King George V shared a happy, loving relationship. Once when she heard the words of a Christmas carol, "Joy to you and all mankind," she told him: "That's you, Grandpa England. You are old and you are very, very kind!"

Passing the Cup At his christening, Prince Charles was given a silver cup by Queen Mary. The cup had originally been given as a christening gift—but not to her—by George III (1760–1820). "I have given a present from my great-grandfather to my great-grandson 168 years later," she noted. Queen Mary is seen in this 1945 photo with her granddaughters, Princesses Elizabeth and Margaret, inspecting a topographical map at the Imperial War Museum.

—*British Information Services*

Earlier Royal Connection The Prince of Wales (future Edward VIII) and his mother, Queen Mary, were godparents to Lord Spencer, the father of Princess Diana.

Q *Name the Queen who was pregnant eighteen times in seventeen years.*

A Queen Anne (1702–14). Her pregnancies from the time she was eighteen until her thirty-fifth birthday (between 1683 and 1700) resulted in thirteen miscarriages or stillbirths. Of her five children who lived, only one survived infancy. All of this happened before she became Queen.

Q *Which Queen was the subject of the children's rhyme, "There Was an Old Woman Who Lived in a Shoe"?*

A Queen Caroline, Consort to George II (1727–60), who gave birth to nine children, one of which was stillborn.

Q *Name the King who was the subject of the children's rhyme, "Georgie Porgie, Pudding and Pie."*

A George I (1714–27).

Q *Which future King said he didn't object to praying to the eternal father but wondered why he had been afflicted with an eternal mother?*

A Edward, Prince of Wales (future Edward VII). His mother, Queen Victoria, ruled for sixty-four years. Edward's reign didn't begin until he was sixty years old.

Q *Which future King once said his mother was the most selfish person he had known?*

A The future George V (1910–36), talking about Queen Alexandra, Consort of Edward VII (1901–10).

End of a Tradition Because of her great love for Prince Albert, Queen Victoria was successful in imposing her desire that all male descendants have his name included in the long list they are given at christening. This linking with the past continued until 1948, when Princess Elizabeth and Prince Philip became the parents of Prince Charles Philip Arthur George.

Four in a Row   The birth of Prince Edward (future Edward VIII) in 1894 marked the first time there were three direct heirs and a living sovereign: Queen Victoria, followed by the future Kings Edward VII, George V, and Edward VIII. A year later yet a fourth future King to the line was born, but at the time nobody could have predicted the Abdication that would bring George VI to the throne. The photo above is also unusual inasmuch as it captures, from left: Queen Consort Mary; the future Queen Elizabeth II holding the present heir presumptive, Prince Charles; and the then reigning Queen Consort Elizabeth, now the Queen Mother.

—British Information Services

Five Generations   When Princess Anne's first child, Peter Mark Andrew Phillips (seen above with his sister Zara in September 1985), was christened in the Music Room at Buckingham Palace in 1977, there were five generations of the royal family present, including Princess Alice, the last surviving grandchild of Queen Victoria. She had been christened at the same gold font in the presence of Queen Victoria ninety-four years earlier. The other four generations were: Elizabeth, the Queen Mother; Elizabeth II; Princess Anne; and young Peter.

—British Information Services

She Has Always Loved Horses   Eighteen-year-old Princess Elizabeth is seen in this 1944 photo at Sandringham, the royal country home, with one of the farm horses. As a young child she once predicted that as Queen she would: "Make a law that there must be no riding on Sundays. Horses should have a rest too." To date she has not.

—*British Information Services*

Both Sides When his parents separated, Prince Philip of Greece was sent to England to be raised by relatives. His four older sisters, meanwhile, married German Princes. In World War II, Philip served in the Royal Navy while his brothers-in-law fought on the side of Germany.

Q *Identify the King who used binoculars to wave to a future Queen nearly every morning.*

A George V enjoyed the morning game from Buckingham Palace with his young granddaughter, the future Elizabeth II, some distance away in her family's home. She, also using binoculars, would wave back.

Q *Which Queen ordered those responsible for training her son to be sure he avoided practical jokes, slang, and dandyism?*

A Queen Victoria, on the rearing of the future Edward VII. Her wishes were woefully predictions of traits he would excell in!

Q *Which Princess had an imaginary friend she talked to called Pinkle Ponkle?*

A Princess Margaret.

Q *What is special about the water used for baptizing royals?*

A By tradition it comes from the River Jordan.

Q *Name the first and last sovereigns to acknowledge the birth of triplets by awarding the parents a monetary gift.*

A The last was Elizabeth II, who discontinued the practice in 1957. It had originated with Queen Victoria, who felt such extraordinary feats deserved royal recognition and authorized the sending of one pound notes to each child.

Q *Which future King did Queen Victoria describe in her diary as dull and ignorant as a child?*

A Her son, the future Edward VII.

Q *Name the Prince of Wales who won a medal for high jumping at school.*

A Prince Charles, at Cheam.

Fact   The royal family can only trace Windsor as the official family name back to the reign of George V (1910–36) during the Great War. Prior to that it had been Saxe-Coburg-Gotha, but George and members of his family thought such an obviously German name might raise questions of his loyalty to Great Britain (there were in fact some nasty whispers), so he changed it to the more Anglo-sounding Windsor. Queen Elizabeth II is seen here seated between her grandparents, King George V and Queen Mary, returning from church.

—*British Information Services*

Royal Titles, Nicknames, and Aliases

Q *What became the official title of Sarah Ferguson once she married Prince Andrew?*

A The Duchess of York. Neither she nor her sister-in-law Diana are princesses in the sense that Princess Anne or Princess Margaret are (by birth).

Q *What title was given to Lady Diana Spencer when she wed Prince Charles?*

A Princess of Wales. Because she is royal only through marriage, her title is dependent on her husband. She had been Lady Diana prior to marriage because her father is an Earl.

Q *What did Princess Margaret's title officially become after marrying Lord Snowdon?*

A Countess of Snowdon.

Q *What are the names of Sarah Ferguson's parents?*

A Her father is Major Ronald Ferguson. Her parents, like those of Princess Diana, are divorced and have both remarried. Her mother, Susan, is married to an Argentine polo player, Hector Barrantes, while her father's second wife is also named Susan.

Q *What is Queen Elizabeth II's full name?*

A Elizabeth Alexandra Mary Windsor.

Fact Princess Diana of Wales, photographed at Kensington Palace by the Earl of Snowdon, can trace her family tree back to King James I and also to his mistress. However, she is not a royal Princess as is her sister-in-law, Anne, or the Queen's sister, Margaret. Diana's title of Princess comes strictly from her husband Charles, Prince of Wales.

—*British Information Services*

Royal Ancestry Although not of royal blood, Sarah Ferguson can trace her ancestry back to King Charles II (1649–85) through the Duke of Buccleuch. She is also related to Queen Elizabeth II through her father, who is a first cousin of Princess Alice, Duchess of Gloucester, widow of the Queen's uncle.

Q *Sarah Margaret Ferguson admitted that as she walked down the aisle to marry Prince Andrew, she was thinking about "ACE." Who is ACE?*

A Albert Christian Edward, the other three names of Prince Andrew which she would have to utter during the ceremony. Fergie remembered that Princess Diana had a bit of confusion with her husband's multiple names on their wedding day and wanted to avoid similar problems. However, since she said "Christian" twice in the ceremony, perhaps she was thinking of ACCE.

Q *Who dropped using her first name, Bessie, because she thought it was "a name given to cows"?*

A Bessie Wallis (also Bessiewallis) Warfield, later Wallis Warfield Spencer, then Wallis Warfield Simpson, and finally the Duchess of Windsor.

Q *Name the cousin of Queen Elizabeth II who was the official photographer at the wedding of Charles and Diana in 1981.*

A The fifth Earl of Lichfield—not to be confused with the Earl of Snowdon. His credits also include nude model layouts for *Playboy* and other U.S. magazines.

Q *Who is known inside the royal family as "Our Val"?*

A Princess Michael of Kent, wife of Prince Michael of Kent. An Austrian, her maiden name was Baroness Marie-Christine von Reibnitz. Servants in Buckingham Palace reportedly spring stiffly to mock military attention in her presence and some members of the family note a Valkyrie-like style, hence the nickname.

Getting Ready Diana, Princess of Wales, made nearly 300 official or public appearances in 1986. Royal-watchers note that the young woman who is now in line to become Queen Consort can expect her appearance schedule only to get heavier as the years go by.

Q What was the Duchess of Kent's name prior to marrying the Duke in June 1961?

A She was Katharine Worsley. The couple were married at York Minster with Princess Anne as one of the young bridesmaids. Photographer Norman Parkinson executed this 1982 portrait.

—British Information Services

Q What is the significance of Princess Anne's four names?

A Elizabeth II's daughter is fully named Anne Elizabeth Alice Louise. The first is the name her great-grandfather nixed when it had been proposed for her aunt, Princess Margaret Rose; her second name is in honor of her mother and grandmother; the third, Alice, is for her father's mother; and the fourth, Louise, is for the Queen of Sweden, who was related to both of her parents. She is seen above arriving at a charity cabaret show to aid the St. John's Ambulance Association, which she is affiliated with.

—British Information Services

Q What is Prince Charles's full title?

A Besides being Prince of Wales, Elizabeth II's son is also: Earl of Chester, Duke of Cornwall, Duke of Rothesay, Earl of Carrick, Baron Renfrew, Lord of the Isles, and Great Steward of Scotland. In addition, the Crown Prince has several honorary titles given by foreign lands and groups in the Commonwealth. This photo shows him wearing the Hunting Stewart kilt at Balmoral Castle, Scotland.

—British Information Services

Question Answered? The answer to the age-old question, "What does a Scotsman wear under his kilt?" may have been answered by Prince Andrew as a youngster. During a family visit to Balmoral, Andrew refused to put on underpants when wearing a kilt. "Papa doesn't wear them!" he announced to staffers who were urging him to step into shorts.

Q *Who was affectionately called "the Wee German Lady"?*

A Queen Victoria, by her good friend and companion in widowhood the Scotsman John Brown. The reference was because Victoria's mother, a German Princess, raised her in heavy German tradition. Her late husband, Prince Albert, was also German.

Q *Which royal child was called "Baby" well into childhood?*

A Princess Beatrice, the youngest child of Queen Victoria. Born in 1858, she lived to see her brother (Edward VII), a nephew (George V), and two great-nephews (Edward VIII and George VI) become King before she died in 1944.

Q *Which Princess was nicknamed Pussy as a child?*

A Queen Victoria's pet name for her first child, and namesake, was Pussy. She was also known as Vicky.

Q *Which royal children nicknamed themselves Toots, Gawks, and Snipey?*

A Princesses Louise, Victoria, and Maud, the three daughters of Albert, Prince of Wales (Edward VII, 1901–10) and Alexandra of Denmark.

Royal Eyeful George III (1760–1820) would not succumb to suggestions that he wear a kilt. His reluctance was bolstered because of an incident that occurred during a reception at St. James' Palace where distinguished men were being received. A Scottish Highlands officer, having been properly announced, approached the king and began to bow deeply. The king immediately noted that the officer's kilt had risen extremely high. Jumping to his feet and waving frantically, George III barked: "Keep the ladies at the back! Keep the ladies at the back!" It took several seconds before the king realized there were no women present.

Q Name the black Labrador Prince Edward posed with on his eighteenth birthday.

A The informal portrait of the Prince, taken at Buckingham Palace on March 10, 1982, was with his dog Frances.

—*British Information Services*

Offensive Wind   In an effort to prevent dogs at the British Embassy in Brazil from passing offensive gas (something they were wont to do with discomforting regularity), the animals' diet was severely restricted for several days prior to a 1968 visit by Elizabeth II. It was never officially reported if the ploy worked.

Q *Which Queen Consort was called "Darling Motherdear" by her children even well after they reached adulthood?*

A Alexandra of Denmark, wife of Edward VII. Though described as "wild as hawks" when young by some visitors, her five children were deeply devoted to her.

Q *What was the full name of Edward, Duke of Windsor?*

A Edward Albert Christian George Andrew Patrick David. He was simply David to the family and very close friends.

Q *When did Elizabeth II become Queen?*

A On February 6, 1952, upon the death of her father, King George VI (1936–52). Her coronation took place on June 2, 1953.

Q *What nickname did Prince Andrew's friends and the press give him because of his eye for women?*

A The Queen's second son was known as Randy Andy in his bachelor days.

Q *Who once publicly called Prince Charles "Fishface"?*

A His wife Diana, during a humorous exchange shortly after they were married.

Just Don't Make Dogs Like They Used To   During an informal dinner hosted by George V and Queen Mary for a small gathering of friends at Balmoral, a sound very much like the passing of wind broke the silence just as the group was entering the dining room. Embarrassed for his guests, the king lashed out with his foot at a frail dog seated near the entranceway. "Filthy brute!" he admonished. Immediately members of the party had to use extraordinary self-control to avoid bursting into laughter. The dog the king had kicked was a lifesize figurine made of fine bone china, and its pieces were scattering all over the place.

Q What does Elizabeth II call her husband in private?
A Like so many wives the world over, the Queen calls him "Darling."

—*British Information Services*

Q What does Prince Charles call his wife?

A "Diana, Love." She, like her mother-in-law, calls her husband "Darling."

—British Information Services

Q What is the full name of Princess Anne, Elizabeth II's daughter?

A She is Anne Elizabeth Alice Louise Windsor Phillips. The Phillips is by marriage to her husband, Mark, while the Windsor is her mother's maiden name rather than her father's family name. Her uncle, the Earl of Snowdon, captured her striking features in this nineteenth-birthday portrait in 1969.

—British Information Services

Hey, Your Majesty, That's Hay During a visit to a country farm in 1891, Queen Victoria asked what were the teepee-style mounds located at intervals throughout the field. It was the first time the seventy-two-year-old monarch had ever seen hay in situ.

Q *What name did Lady Diana use when she went for wedding dress fittings?*

A Deborah Smythson Wells. Her ploy was two-fold: to provide her with privacy, and to protect the dress from any publicity which might risk its being copied.

Q *Identify the royal who sometimes traveled as the Duchess of Balmoral in an effort to secure some degree of privacy.*

A Queen Victoria. The Duchess of Balmoral was one of Victoria's titles.

Q *Which royal identified himself as Edward Bishop while traveling in Italy?*

A Queen Elizabeth II's youngest son, Prince Edward.

Q *Who has used the names Andrew Edwards and Andrew Cambridge in an effort to remain anonymous?*

A Sarah Ferguson's husband, the present Duke of York.

Q *What was Prince Philip's given name at birth?*

A Queen Elizabeth II's future husband was born Philippos Schleswig-Holstein-Sonderberg-Glucksburg. He was a Greek Prince. (Note: he lost his Greek title when he became a British subject in order to marry Princess Elizabeth.)

Q *What is the Queen's official title?*

A Elizabeth the Second, by the Grace of God, of the United Kingdom of Great Britain and Northern Ireland and Her Other Realms and Territories, Queen.

Q *Which member of the royal household is also known as Nambawan Fella?*

A Who else but the person who really is the Number One Fellow, Prince Philip. The nickname is a translation of the pidgin-English name given to Philip by natives in New Guinea.

Fact   When Elizabeth's sister Margaret was born, her parents originally wanted to name her Ann Margaret. However, King George V
disliked the name so much that his grandchild was named Margaret
Rose instead. Princess Margaret Rose is seen here with her parents
and sister on September 7, 1941, the Day of National Prayer, at Crathie
Church near Balmoral Castle.

—*British Information Services*

Security Codenames Much in the same way that the U.S. Secret Service uses codenames when reporting the movements of the President and members of the First Family, and even their destinations, over radio or walkie-talkies, so too do their British counterparts charged with the security of the Queen and the royal family. Elizabeth II and Prince Philip have been signaled as Brenda and Keith, while Prince Charles and Diana have been Brian and Erica. (FYI: Mrs. Lyndon B. Johnson was Victoria in 1978, and for a time during the Carter administration the White House was codenamed Crown by the Secret Service.)

Q *Identify the foreign head of state whom Prince Edward (future Edward VIII) called Uncle Nicky.*

A Nicholas II, Czar of All the Russias (b. 1868–d. 1918). When the Czar visited Osborne Naval College, he was escorted around by his young nephew.

Q *What are the names of Princess Margaret's children?*

A David, Viscount Linley, born in 1961, and Lady Sarah Armstrong-Jones, born in 1964. Their father is the Earl of Snowdon, Anthony Armstrong-Jones. He was given the title upon marrying the Queen's sister.

Q *Who was "Crawfie"?*

A Miss Marion Crawford, the governess who wrote her memoirs after sixteen years of service that included tutoring Princesses Elizabeth and Margaret. The breach of confidence was never forgiven by the royal family.

Q *Which royal, when in a foul mood, is called "Annigoni" by palace servants?*

A Prince Philip. It refers to a stern likeness of him captured by the portrait artist of the same name.

Q *Who were Emma and Satan?*

A A pair of pigs kept as pets when Elizabeth Bowes-Lyon, the Queen Mother, was a child.

Q *What nickname have some palace staffers used to refer to Queen Elizabeth II when she is ill-tempered?*

A Miss Piggy.

Major Family Ties Prince Michael of Kent, born in 1942 and a first cousin of Queen Elizabeth II, was given Franklin as his fourth name in honor of his godfather, President Franklin D. Roosevelt. He is seen in the 1981 photo above, with his wife, wearing the uniform of a major in the Royal Hussars. Princess Michael is the former Marie-Christine von Reibnitz. She is the daughter of a former major in the Nazi SS who was arrested in 1944 and charged with having worked against the Nazis for ten years.

—British Information Services

Legal Protection A British King or Queen cannot be subpoenaed or otherwise requested to testify in court nor can they be sued.

Q *Which member of the royal family was nicknamed Flop by friends at school?*

A Elizabeth II's husband, Prince Philip. Flop was a bit of word play (Philip Flop, as in flip-flop) by his English classmates.

Q *Which member of the royal family was nicknamed Billy the Kid by the press in Australia?*

A Prince William, the young son of Charles and Diana and future Prince of Wales. He is also known as Wee Willie Wales by members of the palace staff.

Q *Who was the first Prince of Wales invested at Caenarvon?*

A Prince Edward (future Edward VIII) in June 1911. The future Duke of Windsor was the first to be invested at a ceremony, despite the 627 years of the title's existence. Previous Princes had simply been proclaimed at Westminster and other English towns. The title of Prince of Wales dates to the year 1284, when King Edward I (1272–1307) presented his baby son to the Welsh people at Caenarvon.

Q *Which member of the royal family dislikes being simply called "Prince"?*

A Charles, who quips: "It makes me sound like a police dog."

Q *What surname did Prince Charles use when he married Lady Diana?*

A None. However, his sister Princess Anne used the surname of Mountbatten-Windsor, which includes both of her parents' names.

Q *What name did Prince Charles and Diana use when booking airline passage home from the Caribbean after a vacation?*

A They were Mr. and Mrs. Hardy.

Q *What was the name of the first horse owned by Prince Andrew?*

A Mr. Dinkum.

Q *What was the name of the rabbit that Prince Charles had as a pet?*

A Harvey, named after the rabbit in the famous play by the same name.

Q What was Charles, Prince of Wales, commonly called by fellow officers during his years in the Royal Navy?

A In keeping with the tradition of using surnames among each other in private, he was simply called Wales. He is seen here in the uniform of a sub-lieutenant, on board HMS *Minerva* in 1974.

—British Information Services

Doubling for a Future King The future George VI convinced a fellow naval college cadet, who bore a remarkable resemblance to him, to take his place from time to time at functions the Prince didn't wish to attend. Once the royal imposter found himself at a ceremony also attended by George V but managed to go undetected.

Q *Which couple used the names Mr. and Mrs. Gordon to mask their identity?*

A Princess Margaret and Tony Armstrong-Jones found it caused less commotion to use the fictitious name when making dinner or theater reservations. After her divorce, Princess Margaret used Mr. and Mrs. Brown when she and Roddy Llewellyn traveled together to the Caribbean.

Q *Identify the member of the royal family who refused to accept the title of Prince of the United Kingdom from King George VI.*

A The soon-to-be husband of Princess Elizabeth, Philip (who technically was not royal at the time). King George VI wanted his daughter, the future Queen, to have a titled husband, and despite Philip's surprising refusal of the King's initial attempt, the King made him Duke of Edinburgh shortly before the wedding. In 1957 Philip became a Prince (again), this time by order of his wife, the Queen.

Q *Which monarch is credited with knighting a piece of beef he found exceptional and thereby creating Sir Loin (sirloin) of Beef?*

A James I and VI.

Q *Which King once wrote an article for print under the name Ralph Robinson?*

A George III (1760–1820), who wrote a paper on agricultural conservation when he was forty-nine years old.

Q *What name did Edward VIII use on his one and only foreign tour as sovereign?*

A The Duke of Lancaster. The trip began August 8, 1936, with a visit to Calais, France, and ended September 14 in Paris before returning to Windsor Great Park. It included several days aboard the *Nahlin*. In all, he and Wallis Warfield Simpson visited eight countries. In telephone conversations with the Duchess before they were married, they identified themselves as James and Janet.

Fact Not everyone in the empire has fully mastered the "Queen's English" and as a result Her Majesty is sometimes known by names one might find a bit surprising. For instance: in New Guinea Elizabeth II is popularly called "Misis Kwin." The Queen is seen above meeting Indian chiefs who gathered to greet her in Calgary, Canada, in 1959.

—*Canada National Film Board photo*

> **Wonerful, Wonerful, Wonerful** During a state visit to France at the invitation of Napoleon III and Empress Eugenie in 1855, Queen Victoria and Prince Albert were dumbstruck at the Paris city hall by a band that played "God Save the Queen." The traditional recognition of the sovereign was done at a polka tempo.

Q *Identify the royal who was given the title "Chief Red Crow" by the Blackfoot Indians of Canada.*

A The eldest son of Elizabeth II, Charles, Prince of Wales.

Q *Which royal was named "Chief Morning Star" by the Stoney Creek Indians of Alberta, Canada?*

A Edward, Prince of Wales (future Edward VIII) during a tour in 1919.

Q *Identify the royal who was given the name "Soya Hun" by the Algonquin Indians.*

A The Duke of York, Prince Andrew. Roughly translated it means "Inheritor of the Lands."

Q *Name the royal who is an honorary Deputy Sheriff in Texas.*

A Prince Philip, but his territory is restricted to Harris County.

Q *What was "the Alexandra Limp"?*

A The name given to the aping of the limp that Queen Alexandra, wife of Edward VII (1901–10), became afflicted with after an illness. Several female Londoners took to including a bit of a limp in their walk for some time afterwards.

Q *Who is recognized as having been the first monarch to be styled King of the English?*

A Ecgbert (829–30), the first of sixteen Anglo-Saxon Kings, the last being (St.) Edward the Confessor (1042–66).

> **Alias, The Prince of Wales** Prince Charles, like other royals, found it convenient to have people think he was someone else at times, and to that end created a number of identities for himself, including: Charles Windsor; Charlie Chester; Mr. Postle; and, on the phone if someone other than Diana answered before they were married, he was Renfrew.

Q Which member of the royal family is also an honorary admiral in the Great Navy of the state of Nebraska?

A The same member who holds the honorary rank of Kentucky Colonel, Prince Philip. However, he was Stroke for this Whaler race crew at Marmarice in Turkey in 1951 while the Royal Navy's Mediterranean Fleet was on its summer cruise.

—*British Information Services*

COMPLETE IN BLOCK LETTERS, PLEASE

SURNAME _____ AGE _9_

CHRISTIAN NAMES ___Anne_____

ADDRESS __Buckingham Palace__

__London S.W.1.__ DATE 8-12-59

I promise to try to remember and keep to the
SAFE RULES OF THE ROAD taught at RoSPA House.

SIGNATURE ___Anne_____

Fact As a young man Prince Philip, like all royals, usually signed papers with only his first name. Once, at a nightclub in London, when politely asked to add his surname while making a reservation, he added "of Greece." To this the receptionist, who obviously didn't recognize him, responded: "A joke is a joke, sir, but that isn't a surname!" In 1959 nine-year-old Princess Anne also simply signed her first name, as seen when she became a member of the Royal Society for the Prevention of Accidents (ROSPA). As she grew older she expanded her signature to P. Anne.

—British Information Services

Q Who was known as "the Wisest Fool in Christendom"?
A James I and VI (1567–1625), the monarch who ordered the first vernacular (English) translation of the Bible.

Q Which two names have been taken by more Kings than any others?
A Henry and Edward, of which there have been eight each.

Q What has been the most frequent name of Queens (and Queen Consorts)?
A Mary and Anne, tied with six each.

Q Which British monarch was the last Emperor of India?
A George VI (1936–52).

Q What was the name of Prince Philip's family home in Corfu, Greece?
A Mon Repos.

The Christmas Tree The German custom of bringing fir trees indoors as the centerpiece for decoration during the Christmas season was introduced in England by the husband of Victoria, Prince Albert.

Q Which royal owned a horse named Bandit?

A Prince Charles, as a child. Actually it was a pony that his sister, Princess Anne, also laid claim to. They are seen riding together some years later in this 1970 photo at Windsor.

—*British Information Services*

Q *Who is the Duke of Lancaster?*

A At present it is Elizabeth II. As such she is acclaimed with the words: To the Queen, The Duke of Lancaster.

Q *Which King had the greatest number of baptismal names?*

A Edward VIII, who was christened Edward Albert Christian George Andrew Patrick David. Additionally he had the titles: Prince Edward; Prince of Wales; Prince Edward of York; Prince Edward of Cornwall; and Duke of Cornwall. After the Abdication he became the Duke of Windsor. Within the family he was simply known as David.

Q *Identify the Queen with the greatest number of baptismal names.*

A Queen Mary (May of Teck, Consort of George V, 1910–36). Her actual first name wasn't May or Mary but rather Victoria. She was baptized Victoria Mary Augusta Louisa Olga Pauline Claudine Agnes.

Q *Which Queen called her clothes her props?*

A Elizabeth, the Queen Mother, Consort to George VI (1936–52), who believed royals had to dress and look the part the same way performers do when before an audience.

Q *Which royal couple called official functions and obligatory parties they disliked "Bore Hunts"?*

A The pair that were on everybody's invitation list, the Duke and Duchess of Windsor.

Q *Which royal is credited with nicknaming champagne "Boy"?*

A Edward, Prince of Wales (future Edward VII). It reportedly began during a trip to Germany when he called "Boy" to attract the young man serving champagne. Since it was fashionable to follow Edward's lead, others in the party began holding up empty glasses and calling for "Boy."

Q *Which royal called Buckingham Palace "the House in Pimlico"?*

A George V (1910–36), for reasons unknown.

Royal Identification   As a child, Prince Charles could hardly contain himself whenever he heard his name read from the pulpit in church and more than once cried out to the embarrassment of his mother, "That's me, Mummy!"

Q What were the names of the two Corgis Elizabeth II had when she
became Queen?

A Sugar and Susan were the favored two at the time. Over the years
she has had other pet Corgis, including this pair which accompanied
her to Scotland in 1970.

—British Information Services

> **Her Favorite Things** Elizabeth II is partial to: Corgi dogs; horses; carnations; Dick Francis novels; Chinese teas; chocolate mints; and fruit salads. She doesn't like: cats; escargots; caviar; oysters; or heights.

Q *What are the Queen's dorgis?*
A Mixbreeds born as a result of an assignation between one of her Corgis and a Dachshund belonging to Princess Margaret.

Q *What was the name of the first Corgi owned by Queen Elizabeth?*
A Dookie; she received the pet as a child.

Q *Name the pet of Edward VII (1901–10) that was photographed following his remains during the King's funeral.*
A His dog Caesar.

Q *Which King called his wife "the Dutch Cow"?*
A Henry VIII (1509–47) used the term, referring to his fourth wife, Anne, daughter of the Duke of Cleves, and it is one of the kinder things he said about her. The marriage had been arranged for political opportunity with Henry only having seen paintings of Anne. So different did she look from the flattering portraits that Henry at their first meeting turned to his envoys and asked them if they had brought him the Flanders Mare (a horse). Political winds changed and Henry rid himself of Anne in six months.

Q *Who was nicknamed "William the Conqueror, the traveling salesman of Britain"?*
A Prince William, son of the Duke of Gloucester, by *The Australian Woman's Weekly* in 1945. The young Prince's father had been posted to Australia as Governor General. History would repeat itself in 1983 when William, Prince of Wales (son of Charles and Diana), received the same nickname during a visit Down Under.

> **Going, Going . . . Still Here!** During the first twenty years of her reign (1952–72), there were no less than seventy-one separate newspaper and magazine stories printed worldwide predicting the immediate abdication of Elizabeth II. Ill health, marital problems, and the desire to lead a "normal" life were the most frequent reasons cited.

Fact When Philip of Greece relinquished his foreign title to become a British subject, his name was formally changed to Philip Mountbatten. This was the surname of his mother. Philip himself considered taking Oldcastle as a surname. In January 1957, during his Antarctica tour, he took time to make friends with some local inhabitants at the Penguin Rookery Base east of Adelaide Island.

—*British Information Services*

Buying a Title   The fifth Earl of Lichfield, a cousin of Elizabeth II, caused Her Majesty some distress a few years ago when he auctioned off four of his minor titles for the total sum of $67,000. Lichfield, called Patrick by close friends, once dated movie actress Britt Ekland and reportedly earns $450,000 per year from his photography business.

Q *Which royal has the title Lord of Man?*

A Elizabeth II, because one of her protectorates is the Isle of Man.

Q *By what title is Prince Charles known in Scotland?*

A The Duke of Rothesay. The title, the highest given to the heir to the British throne, was created by Robert III of Scotland (1390–1406) for his son David in 1398. Rothesay is the chief town of the county and island of Bute.

Q *Which Queen was nicknamed Duck by her grandson?*

A Queen Victoria. The grandson was the child of her daughter, Princess Royal Victoria. He grew up to be the German Kaiser, Wilhelm II (b. 1895–d. 1941).

Q *Who is known in palace circles as Charlie's Aunt?*

A Princess Margaret, Duchess of Snowdon, the aunt of Prince Charles.

Q *Of whom was the Duke of Windsor (former Edward VIII) speaking when he referred to "the Fat Scotch Cook"?*

A His sister-in-law, the woman who was Queen Consort to George VI, Elizabeth Bowes-Lyon, the Queen Mother. Friends have said that the spiteful nickname actually originated with the Duchess of Windsor, who for years considered herself Queen Consort to the real King.

Q *Of whom are the present royal family members speaking when they refer to "the Bicycle Royals"?*

A The Scandinavian royals, who are known to enjoy riding bikes on the same streets and roads as common folk.

Q *Who was known as "the Pompous Bastard" by those students who resented him at school?*

A Prince Charles. The school where the nickname hatched was Timbertops in Australia.

Q Which member of the royal family was once voted Sportswoman of the Year?

A Princess Anne, in 1971, because of her enthusiasm and equestrian abilities. She is seen above competing in a 1970 show-jumping event at Eridge Park.

—*British Information Services*

Fact   It is not unusual for guests of the Queen to find the after-dinner conversation turning to horses. She enjoys sharing the subject so much that she has, at times, asked guests to help select names for newly born thoroughbreds. Provided with the names of the sire and dam, guests are asked to use this information to come up with appropriate names. Some have included: Pall Mall (from Malapert and Palestine); Royal Taste (from Kingstone and Saucy Lass); and Stenographer (from Fair Copy and Saucy Lass). The Queen is seen here on the track at Ascot giving one of her horses a good run.

—British Information Services

Q What is the official title of Prince Philip?

A Elizabeth II's husband is His Royal Highness the Prince Philip, Duke of Edinburgh, Earl of Merioneth, and Baron of Greenwich. In the 1953 photo above, he is at the controls of the Vickers Viscount 700 prototype, which he piloted for some thirty minutes.

—*British Information Services*

> **It Beats Just Playing a Hunch**   So consuming is Elizabeth II's interest in horses and desire to win the Derby, the greatest horse race in Britain, that she files breeding and racing statistics in a computer given to her by President Ronald Reagan. In recent years she has also sent choice mares to Kentucky to be mated with U.S. horses.

Q *Which royal, like hundreds of others his age who wore braces, was nicknamed Jaws at school?*

A Prince Edward, at Gordonstoun. In 1986, after graduation from Cambridge, he was assigned to a year of commando training with the Marines and was promptly nicknamed "the Royal Rambo" in the press.

Q *Who was Prince Charles's governess?*

A Miss Catherine Peebles, whom he called Mispy (Miss P.).

Q *Which royal was chosen captain of the school hockey team?*

A Diana, Princess of Wales.

Q *Who was nicknamed "the Fuehrer" by the Queen Mother?*

A Peter Cazalet, the strict former trainer of the royal family horses.

Q *Who called Edward, Prince of Wales (future Edward VIII) Peter Pan?*

A The man who lost his wife to the King who lost his throne for her: Ernest Simpson.

Q *Who was known as Seven-Eighths?*

A The Duchess of Windsor, while still Wallis Warfield Spencer Simpson during the Abdication crisis. Her future husband was, at the time, Edward VIII. Insiders felt she would never be Queen and so fell short of inheriting Edward's Roman Numeral title. Thus she was seven-eighths instead of a full VIII.

Q *Which Prince of Wales was nicknamed "the Baker" by employees of his mistress?*

A The future Edward VIII, who was romantically involved with Mrs. Dudley Ward for sixteen years. The reference was to the fact that the Prince, like the vendor who brought fresh loaves, arrived on time each morning.

Q What was the actual first name of George VI?

A Albert, though his wife and members of the family called him Bertie. He took the name George as King in honor of his late father, George V.

—National Portrait Gallery

A Rose By Any Other Name   George VI once ordered a gardener to stop addressing him as "Your Royal Highness." "I'm sick of hearing it all day! You may call me that only once each day . . . and no more." To which the gardener responded, "Yes, Your Royal Highness."

Q *Identify the Queen whom a foreign royal nicknamed after an Oliver Twist character because he felt she had a jewel that belonged to his country.*

A Queen Victoria, who was sometimes called Mrs. Fagin by the Maharajah of Punjab. The jewel in dispute was the Koh-i-noor Diamond.

Q *What is a Queen Anne Fan?*

A The same thing we call a "raspberry" in America: thumb to nose, fingers fluttering, tongue stuck out, accompanied by a crude sound. Origin unknown.

Q *Whom did Queen Victoria call "that Italian Electrician"?*

A Guglielmo Marconi, the inventor of the wireless radio, whom she thought was a commoner who didn't know his place. Her indignation originated when she had him summoned to set up receiving and sending stations between the royal yacht and Osborne House, her island residence, during a period when the Prince of Wales was convalescing from a knee injury. When she learned Marconi had crossed a garden reserved for her use while he was inspecting the work of his installers, she was furious and ordered, "Get another electrician." To which an aide responded, "Alas, Your Majesty, England has no Marconi." Ironically, Marconi was knighted by George V some years later for his pioneering work in the communication field.

Q *Name the royal who once called Mark Phillips, Princess Anne's husband, "Fog" ("because he is thick, and wet").*

A Her loving brother, Prince Charles.

Q *Name the King who called his family "the Firm."*

A George VI (1936–52).

Q *What did Edward, Duke of Kent, call his young daughter, the future Queen Victoria, as a child?*

A Drina, a short form of her actual first name, Alexandrina.

Q What is the oldest of the Christian orders of chivalry?

A The Most Noble Order of the Garter, founded in 1348 by Edward III (1327–77). In this June 1968 photo, Prince Charles wears a blue velvet mantle and plumed cap in the procession of the Garter Knights to St. George's Chapel, Windsor, where he was installed as a Knight Companion of the Order by Queen Elizabeth II.

—British Information Services

Q What year was the Most Noble Order of the Garter established?

A It dates from 1348. Each year new Knights are admitted in an annual ceremony at Garter Chapel in Windsor Castle. Queen Elizabeth II and Prince Philip are seen in this June 1960 photo in procession from Victoria Tower to that year's ceremony. The honor is conferred in recognition of distinguished public service.

—*British Information Services*

Q *Which future sovereign called George IV (1820–30) Uncle King?*
A His niece, the future Queen Victoria.

Q *Name the royal who was known at school as Bat Lugs because of his large ears.*
A George VI, at Dartmouth.

Q *Which King's death resulted in the "throne" becoming a slang nickname for the toilet seat?*
A George II (1727–60), who suffered a coronary and died while sitting on the toilet. Detractors found humor in the comparison, which is still used today.

Q Who frequently called King Charles II (1660–85) Charles III?
A Nell Gwynne, above, perhaps his most famous mistress. She reasoned that since two of her previous lovers had also been named Charles, the numerical designation was appropriate.

—British Museum

American Namesakes Several cities, towns, villages, and entire colonies in pre-Revolutionary America were named after British royalty. The following continued their names as states:

Georgia ....George II
Maryland .... Henrietta Maria, wife of Charles I
New York .... Duke of York, future Charles I
North Carolina .... Charles II
South Carolina .... Charles I
Virginia .... Elizabeth, the Virgin Queen

Q *Who was Bloody Mary?*

A Queen Mary I (1553–58), the daughter of Henry VIII (1509–47), who had a penchant for prosecuting Protestants in her efforts to restore Roman Catholicism to England. She was the first Queen to rule England in her own right and the only reigning Queen to marry a foreign reigning King, Philip II of Spain.

Q *Name the only Queen to name her Consort as joint sovereign.*

A Mary II (1689–94), who was outlived by William III (1689–1702).

Q *Which King was known as the Merry Monarch?*

A Charles II (1660–85), because of his extremely active libido. He acquired his first mistress, the wife of the Governor of Bridgewater, at age fifteen. Over the years he added a chaplain's daughter, a few duchesses, a bridesmaid at his wedding, and at least two actresses, Nell Gwynne and Moll Davis.

Q *Which royal earned the name "Brandy Nan" because of her heavy drinking?*

A Queen Anne (1702–14).

Q *Which King was referred to as "My fat friend" by Beau Brummell?*

A George IV (1820–30).

Q *Who was known as Tum-tum?*

A King Edward VII, who followed his mother, Queen Victoria, to the throne when he was sixty years old. Edward VII ranks high among monarchs with large appetites. He earned the nickname because of the rotund appearance he acquired living the good life as Prince of Wales.

Name This Tank! During her first foreign visit alone in 1969, Colonel-in-Chief Princess Anne had an opportunity to drive a 52-ton Chieftain tank for three miles over some rather rough country in Germany while visiting "her" regiment, 14th, 20th King's Hussars. Name of the tank? Why, *Princess Anne*, naturally.

—British Information Services

Security After the Duke of Windsor died in 1972, the Duchess slept with a gun near her pillow for several years. His brother, George VI, reportedly kept a Sten gun nearby at all times.

Q *Which royal was named "Hooligan of the Year" in 1978?*

A Prince Charles, whose hunting exploits offended the Royal Society for the Prevention of Cruelty to Animals.

Q *Name the male royal who was honored for having done the most to promote tasteful hairstyles in 1973.*

A Captain Mark Phillips, who won the title the year he married Princess Anne.

Q *Identify the royal who was selected the Best Dressed Man of 1954.*

A The then five-year-old Prince Charles. The "award" was given by a British fashion industry magazine.

Q *Who is the only Archbishop of Canterbury to have crowned three Kings?*

A Archbishop Thomas Cardinal Bourchier (b. 1412–d. 1486). The Kings were: Edward IV (1461–83); Richard III (1377–99); and Henry VII (1485–1509). (See related box in Appendix, p. 234.)

Q *Who is the only King to have been crowned in both England and France?*

A Henry VI (1422–61 and 1470–71). Henry was eight months old at the time of his succession to the British throne after the death of his father, Henry V (1413–22), and one month later he was proclaimed King of France upon the death of his maternal grandfather, Charles VI. Seven years later, in 1429, he was crowned King of England in Westminster Abbey and in 1431 King of France at Notre Dame.

Q *Identify the only two of Henry VIII's six wives who were crowned Queen.*

A His first, Catherine, and second, Anne Boleyn, whom he had executed. His other wives were never afforded the honor of coronations.

Q *How many Kings were named Stephen?*

A One (1135–54), the first and last of that name. He had been Count of Mortain and Count of Boulogne. His wife's name was Matilda.

Q Who was Thelma Vanderbilt?

A The woman who introduced Edward, Prince of Wales, to the future Duchess of Windsor, Wallis Warfield Simpson. Her twin sister is Gloria Vanderbilt. Also an American who married royalty (she was Lady Furness), Thelma Vanderbilt had herself been romantically involved with the Prince of Wales until she introduced him to Mrs. Simpson, seen above in this 1934 photo by Cecil Beaton. (Diana, Princess of Wales, can trace a family relationship to the Vanderbilt sisters (see Appendix: Princess Diana's Famous Ancestors).

—photo by Cecil Beaton

Royal Quotes,
Letters, Messages

Q *Which King showed his displeasure during a church sermon by shouting back at a minister: "I give not a turd for your preaching!"?*
A The outspoken James I and VI (1567–1625).

Q *Who gave the following explanation for returning the office of Member of the British Empire (MBE) to the Queen: "I don't believe in royalty and titles"?*
A John Lennon in 1969. The former Beatle said the MBE was "an embarrassment to me. It was a humiliation."

Q *What were Prince Charles's first words to Princess Diana at the altar on their wedding day?*
A "You look wonderful!" and she replied, "Wonderful for you."

Q *"I am not your 'love.' I am Your Royal Highness!" Which member of the royal family snapped these words at a photographer who tried to get her attention with the command: "Look this way, love"?*
A The daughter of Elizabeth II, Princess Anne, during a trip to Australia.

Q *Which Princess quipped, "I'm not Mrs. Thatcher," when asked by a photographer to pose holding a toy during a children's party?*
A Princess Anne, in 1979.

Didn't Take Him Seriously When a bishop, after the death of Prince Albert in 1861, suggested to the forty-two-year-old Queen Victoria that she should thereafter consider herself "as married to Christ," confusion immediately registered on the Queen's face. After a long silence during which a sarcastic smile briefly twisted her lip, she looked squarely at the bishop and replied: "That's what I call twaddle!"

Q What television show does the Queen Mother watch to learn what life is like for commoners?

A "My favorite program is 'Mrs. Dale's Diary.' I try never to miss it." She is seen above in the official portrait taken for her fiftieth birthday, August 4, 1950.

—*British Information Services*

Abdication Prediction From the book by Nostradamus entitled *Centuries,* published in 1555, comes the following prophecy which is said to refer to Edward VIII and George VI: "For being unwilling to consent to divorce/Which later shall be recognized as unworthy/ The King of the Isles shall be expelled by force/And replaced by one whose nature will not be that of King." History records that George VI was reluctant to replace his brother.

Q *Who described the wedding of Princess Anne and Captain Mark Phillips as: "Pure operetta, the best of Strauss . . . but all the characters are for real"?*

A Norman Parkinson, the official wedding photographer.

Q *Which royal wanted a wedding "like something out of* Cinderella"?

A Sarah, Duchess of York, who got her wish in July 1986 when she and Prince Andrew were married.

Q *Who said: "They'll pay anything to see us"?*

A Princess Margaret, to her sister Princess Elizabeth in 1941 while they were preparing for *Cinderella,* a Christmas play. Margaret had suggested that the audience of family and friends be charged for the performance. Elizabeth doubted anyone would come if they had to pay. Pay they did.

Q *Of whom was Winston Churchill speaking when he said theirs "was one of the greatest love stories of history"?*

A Edward VIII and Wallis Warfield Simpson, later the Duke and Duchess of Windsor.

Q *Who called the romance and eventual Abdication of Edward VIII for the love of Wallis Simpson "the greatest story since the Crucifixion"?*

A American journalist H. L. Mencken.

Q *Who once called herself "the greatest whore in the world"?*

A Giulia Barucci, a mistress of the Prince of Wales (future Edward VII) until he was thirty years old.

Q *Who said: "A woman can never be too rich or too thin"?*

A The Duchess of Windsor.

Q Who said the following about Princess Margaret: "She isn't really a rose, just a bud"?

A Her four-year-old sister, the future Queen Elizabeth II, after seeing new-born Margaret for the first time. The princess is seen here taking leave of the queen, the *Delta Queen,* for a port call during a November 1986 one-week river cruise aboard the second largest steamboat ever built. Jimmy Coleman, left, Honorary British Consul for Louisiana and D. Perry Moran, right, vice president of Delta Queen Steamboat Co., are seen escorting her.

—*Delta Queen Steamboat Co. photo*

Confederate Relative *A Connecticut Yankee in King Arthur's Court* may have been interesting reading but there is no fiction in the fact that Elizabeth II can include a Confederate general in her ancestral court. She is a descendant of Colonel Augustine Warner, a Virginian, whose daughter Sarah was great-great-great-grandmother of General Robert E. Lee. Sarah's brother had a daughter, Mary, and it was Mary's great-great-great-great-granddaughter who became the grandmother of Elizabeth II.

Q *Who said the following about Princess Diana: "Ask me about her beautiful blue eyes"?*

A Prime Minister Pierre Trudeau of Canada in 1983, who had obviously been taken by her good looks and charm during the royal tour.

Q *Who reported that Prince Charles had "looked long and hard down my cleavage" during a state visit?*

A Margaret Trudeau, former wife of the Prime Minister of Canada.

Q *Which royal once described herself as having "tiny boobs and big shoulders"?*

A Princess Michael of Kent.

Q *Who described Queen Alexandra, the wife of Edward VII, as being "flat as a board"?*

A Her mother-in-law, Queen Victoria.

Q *Name the Prince who commented on royal training with the remark: "I've learnt the way a monkey learnt, by watching its parents."*

A Prince Charles.

Q *Who said: "The boy will ruin himself within twelve months"?*

A King George V, shortly before his death. He was referring to his son, Prince Edward, who would follow him to the throne but then renounce it within the year for the woman he loved.

Q *Which royal was described by crew members of a ferry as an "upper-class hooligan" because of the way he and his associates carried on during a 1981 trip?*

A Mark Phillips, husband of Princess Anne, who with his friends had reportedly sprayed champagne and generally acted wild on board.

Royal Jester   During the final rehearsal for Prince Andrew and Sarah Ferguson's wedding, his twenty-two-year-old brother, Prince Edward, showed up with his left arm in a sling. This immediately set off speculation as to whether he would be able to function properly as best man. Then it was observed that Prince Edward had switched the sling to his right arm. "Just a joke," a deadpan Buckingham Palace spokesman announced afterwards. Prince Edward is seen above in a November 1982 photo.

—British Information Services

Royal Rich Little? When George IV (1820–30) was Prince Regent, he often caused close friends to go into guarded howls of laughter with his impersonations of his father, George III. A favorite routine was the King reading the American Declaration of Independence and asking for translations of "Liberty" and "the pursuit of Happiness."

Q *Which royal asked her doctor: "Can I have no more fun in bed?"*

A Queen Victoria, upon being told she could, or should, no longer become pregnant.

Q *Who said: "If men had to have babies, they would only have one each."*

A Princess Diana.

Q *Name the royal who commented that pregnancy was "What we're made for."*

A Princess Elizabeth (future Elizabeth II), responding to a question while carrying Prince Charles.

Q *Which royal said pregnancy was a "penalty" for being a woman?*

A Princess Mary of Teck, wife of George, Prince of Wales (future George V).

Q *Identify the royal who called being pregnant an "occupational hazard of being a wife."*

A Princess Anne.

Q *Which royal was "furious" at discovering she was pregnant?*

A Queen Victoria. She made the statement in her later years to her eldest child, Princess Royal Victoria Adelaide (whom she was "furious" about!), as Vicky prepared for marriage.

Q *Who said the following about childbirth: "It's not a duty because I'm not a boy"?*

A Princess Anne, who enjoyed three years of married life before the birth of her first child.

Q *Who said: "If children are too strictly or perhaps severely treated they only fear those whom they ought to love"?*

A Albert, Prince of Wales (future Edward VII).

Royal Humor When she was a Second Subaltern in the Auxiliary Territorial Service during World War II, the future Queen Elizabeth II was victim of a prank played by her father, George VI. She was learning automobile mechanics in 1944 when, during a visit, the King removed the distributor from a car she was attempting to get started as part of her final test. After a good laugh he told her the reason the vehicle failed to start. She replaced it and passed easily. In photo above, Elizabeth relates the story to Princess Margaret.

—*British Information Services*

Anything For a Laugh Edward VII was perhaps the sovereign with the oddest sense of humor. He was keen on placing lobsters, birds, mice, worms, dried peas, and various other things in the beds of house guests. The results of these antics were described by an observer: "If anyone caught his foot on a mat, or nearly fell into the fire or out of a window, the mirth of the whole royal family knew no bounds."

Q *Which royal had the following question concerning morning sickness during pregnancy: "Why did no one tell me you felt like this?"*

A Princess Diana, who experienced severe morning sickness with her first child.

Q *Which royal describes herself as "not particularly maternal in outlook"?*

A Princess Anne, who reportedly enjoys the kind of lifestyle her mother the Queen always wanted.

Q *Who said: "An ugly baby is a very nasty object"?*

A Queen Victoria, whose love for her own children never clouded her frankness. She added: "and the prettiest is frightful when undressed, till about four months." Some years later she would write of her hemophiliac son, Prince Leopold: "He is very ugly, I think uglier even than he was."

Q *Who said: "The children are so pleased with the baby who they think flew in at my window and had to have his wings cut off!"?*

A The Duchess of York, Princess May, and future Queen Mary, in a letter to her aunt Augusta reporting the birth of her third son, Henry, in 1900.

Q *Who said the following about the Abdication of Edward VIII: "If he had stayed, everything would have been different. His abdication was a severe loss for us"?*

A Adolf Hitler, to his Armaments Minister Albert Speer and others during the planning of Operation Sea Lion, the proposed invasion of England.

Q *Did Adolf Hitler once describe the future Queen Elizabeth II as "a marvelous child"?*

A Yes. He also often had nice things to say about her aunt, the Duchess of Windsor.

Q Who said: "A good suit goes on forever"?

A Princess Anne, seen here with her future husband, Lieutenant Mark Phillips, the day after their engagement was announced. She is wearing a suit with a pleated tartan underlay and matching bow tie.

—British Information Services

Waste Not, Want Not   Elizabeth II is said to have sequins, beads, and other such items removed from garments she no longer cares to wear and then reapplied to newer clothes.

Q *Did Queen Alexandra, Consort of George V, make the following comment on the romance between Edward VIII and Mrs. Simpson: "We did it better in my day"?*

A No. Queen Alexandra accepted the fact that her husband had a mistress and the quote has erroneously appeared in print several times as her failure to understand why Edward VIII couldn't have stayed on the throne and kept Mrs. Simpson as a mistress. But Alexandra died on November 20, 1925, five years before Edward and Mrs. Simpson even met and eleven years before the Abdication crisis.

Q *Who said: "Either the brute is a King or else he is an ordinary black nigger, and if he is not a King, why is he here at all?"*

A Edward VII, while still Prince of Wales, in a rebuff to objections raised by his German relatives, who were offended that the Hawaiian King, Kalakaua (1874–81), had been assigned what was considered a better place at an official dinner than Edward's grand-nephew, Crown Prince William (1882–1951) of Germany.

Q *Identify the royal who considered the American Apollo space program a "waste of money."*

A Prince Philip, during a visit to Brazil in 1968. The remark came less than a month after the first manned launch in the program, Apollo 7, and a month before the historic Christmas Eve circumnavigation of the moon by Astronauts Frank Borman, Jim Lovell, and Bill Anders in Apollo 8.

Q *"You married my father!" Who said it to whom, and why?*

A Prince Charles, to his new bride, Diana, after she had nervously transposed his name during the ceremony. She should have said: "Charles Philip Arthur George," but instead it came out: "Philip Charles Arthur George."

Q *Who described Queen Elizabeth II at her accession in 1952 thus: "A fair and youthful figure, Princess, wife and mother, is the heir to all our glories and traditions"?*

A Winston S. Churchill.

Weighty Conversation   On the eve of her wedding to Prince Andrew, Sarah Ferguson commented publicly about her weight for the
first time: "I do not diet . . . I do not have a problem. A woman should
have a trim waist, a good 'up top' and enough down the bottom, but
not too big . . . a good womanly figure." For several months previously
a number of tabloid newspapers had speculated on her measurements.

—*British Information Services*

She Never Heard of Queen Anne   Queen Victoria, who found it difficult to believe there really were male homosexuals, was totally unable to accept the fact that there was such a thing as lesbians. When an anti-homosexual law was passed by Parliament, she refused to sign it until references to sex acts between females were removed.

Q *Who said: "I love the Queen, perhaps the only person in the world left to me that I do love"?*
A Benjamin Disraeli, talking about Queen Victoria.

Q *Who said: "I have to tell you, Queen Elizabeth [II] is a most charming, down-to-earth person. Incidentally, she's a very good rider"?*
A The President of the United States, Ronald Reagan.

Q *Of whom was the Queen Mother speaking when she said: "What a pity. We were saving her for Charles"?*
A Lady Leonora Grosvenor, shortly after it was publicly announced that Lady Leonora and the fifth Earl of Lichfield were engaged to be married in the mid-1970s. Lady Leonora, a lady-in-waiting to Charles's sister Princess Anne, filed for divorce from Lichfield in July 1986.

Q *Who wished newspaper reporters: "A Happy New Year and your editors a particularly nasty one"?*
A Prince Charles, when he was courting Lady Diana and discovered the press at every turn.

Q *Who said: "That's the most pompous thing I have ever heard" to a newspaper editor?*
A Queen Elizabeth II, responding to the question: "Why can't the Princess [Diana] send a servant to buy her winegums?" The exchange took place at a press conference the Queen called to ask the press to give the newly married couple some privacy, pointing out that Diana could not even walk to a village shop without being harassed. Another reported version of the incident has the Queen saying: "What a pompous remark, if I may say so."

Q *Who said: "The reign of King George VI is a split-level matriarchy in pants. Queen Mary runs the King's wife [Queen Elizabeth], and the King's wife runs the King!"?*
A The Duchess of Windsor, quoted in the book *The Windsor Story*.

Q What year did Queen Elizabeth II make her first Christmas broadcast?
A In 1952.

—British Information Services

Escape Route   A special underground tunnel connects Buckingham Palace to the railway system and Heathrow Airport. It is intended for use by the royal family in the event of war.

Q *Which King wrote the following to his wife on their seventeenth wedding anniversary: "My love grows stronger for you every day mixed with admiration and I thank God every day that he has given me such a darling, devoted wife as you are"?*

A George V, to Queen Mary in 1910.

Q *Who said: "I shall soon have a regiment, not a family"?*

A King George V, whose eldest son, the Duke of Windsor, had no children and whose youngest child died in adolescence. However, the four remaining came close to fulfilling his wish: From his second son, George VI, descend Queen Elizabeth II and Princess Margaret and their children (and in the Queen's case grandchildren); from Princess Mary and Princes Henry and George descend the Harewoods, Gloucesters, and Kents.

Q *Who said: "What does it matter if I am killed? I have four brothers"?*

A Edward, Prince of Wales (future Edward VIII), in earnestly seeking to be sent to the front lines during the Great War. The question was asked of Lord Kitchener and other officials at the War Office whom Edward thought would be cooperative toward his request.

Q *Who said: "Sirs, will you kill your King? I am your King, I your captain and your leader"?*

A Richard II (1377–99), addressing the angry crowd bent on violence in the Peasants' Revolt of 1381. His words worked and the revolt was ended.

Q *Who said: "Alas, I would my uncle would let me have my life yet, though I lose my Kingdom"?*

A The twelve-year-old uncrowned King Edward V (1483), who with his brother Richard became known as the Princes in the Tower (of London).

Q *Who said: "For better or for worse, royalty is excluded from the more settled forms of domesticity"?*

A The Duke of Windsor.

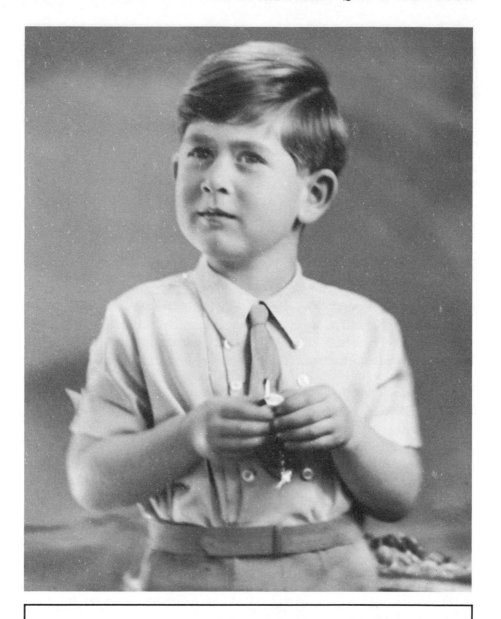

Q Who was the recipient of postcards inscribed "WITH LOVE FROM CHARLES" shortly after he learned to write the alphabet in capital letters?

A His parents, Elizabeth II and Prince Philip, while they were in Australia and New Zealand in 1953. The young Prince is seen here in his official fifth-birthday portrait, November 14, 1953, a few days before his parents left on the Royal Tour.

—British Information Services

Warning—No Wet Paint   In an effort to spruce up buildings whenever a royal visit is expected, fresh coats of paint are usually added to exteriors, interiors, and just about anything else in sight, much to the dismay of Prince Charles, who dislikes the smell of fresh paint: "It sticks in my nose and makes me feel nauseous. Why do people paint everything when I am due somewhere?"

Q *Identify the child who said the following to a governess after having been difficult: "I'm very sorry . . . but I mean to be just as naughty again"?*

A Vicky, the Princess Royal, eldest child of Queen Victoria. She reportedly spent considerable time restricted to her room as a youngster because of her behavior.

Q *Name the Princess who responded by saying: "But she likes it, my dear," to her mother (the Queen) when warned that a particular food wasn't good for her.*

A Princess Beatrice, youngest of Queen Victoria's nine children. She then went ahead and ate the disputed food.

Q *Which Prince of Wales caused his tutor to make the following diary entry: "The P. of W. has been like a person half silly. I could not gain his attention. He was very rude, particularly in the afternoon, throwing stones in my face"?*

A The ten-year-old son of Queen Victoria, Prince Albert Edward, later Edward VII.

Q *Who said: "Never mind, the next will be a Prince," when told by the attending doctor that her firstborn was a Princess?*

A Queen Victoria, in 1840, immediately after the birth of Princess Royal Victoria (Vicky). And so it was, for within a year she had a son, Albert (Bertie), Prince of Wales, named after his father, but who became Edward VII.

Q *Which royal had the following as a guiding principle in her wishes for her children: "That they should be brought up as simply as possible and that they should be as often as possible with their parents . . . "?*

A Queen Victoria, who with her husband, Albert, enjoyed music, gardening, sailing, and numerous other activities with their children.

Q Which royal said that in most cases fourth children are unintentional?

A Prince Philip, the father of four children, the last of whom was Prince Edward, born when Elizabeth II was thirty-eight years old and seen above in his twenty-first-birthday portrait on March 10, 1985.

—*British Information Services*

Shake, Pal During his 1919 overseas tour, which included a visit to Canada, the future Edward VIII was approached by a man who extended a hand in greeting, saying: "Put it right here, Ed. I shook hands with your granddad." Within a week the Prince of Wales shook so many hands that his own became black and swollen.

Q *Which one does Queen Elizabeth II call "the quietest of my children"?*

A Prince Edward, her youngest, born in 1964.

Q *Who said: "The greatest advantage of my entire life is the family I grew up in"?*

A Princess Anne, who added: "I am eternally thankful for being able to grow up in the sort of atmosphere that was given to me . . . the family was always there."

Q *Who said: "My children are not royal, they just happen to have an aunt who is Queen"?*

A Princess Margaret, in making the point that her children's lives would be much different to the lives of her sister's children.

Q *Who said being Consort was "the hardest job in the world"?*

A King George VI, shortly before Prince Philip's marriage to Princess Elizabeth: "Philip's the right man for Lilibet but I don't think he realizes what he's letting himself in for. One day Lilibet will be Queen and he will be consort. And that's the hardest job in the world."

Q *Who said: "The position of the Prince Consort requires that the husband should entirely sink his own individual existence in that of his wife"?*

A Prince Albert, husband of Queen Victoria.

Q *Who said: "Australia conquered my shyness"?*

A Prince Charles, who spent two school terms there and mixed well with fellow students, who were interested but not in awe of him.

Q *Who said the following about Elizabeth, the Queen Mother: "Ever since I can remember [she] has been the most wonderful example of fun, laughter, warmth, infinite security and, above all else, exquisite taste . . . "?*

A Prince Charles, her grandson, in 1979.

Q Who said the following about his children's names: "It makes them sound like bastards"?

A Prince Philip, reacting to a royal decree by his wife that reverted her name and that of her children (Charles and Anne at the time) to her maiden name of Windsor in place of her husband's name, Mountbatten. He added that the change also made him just "a bloody amoeba." The royal quartet is seen at Balmoral Castle, Scotland, in 1955. Princes Andrew and Edward, born later, have hyphenated surnames: Mountbatten-Windsor.

—British Information Services

But Why Is 12 Inches a "Ruler"?   Henry I (1100–35), the Lion of Justice, determined the unit of measurement called a yard by measuring the distance between his nose and his right thumb (the distance to his left thumb was a fraction shorter).

Q *Who said: "I decided my children should never be allowed to see more than three great pictures at a time"?*

A Princess Margaret, who as a child herself had been "absolutely exhausted" by hours of walking and standing in museums. She determined that it would be better for her own children to plead to see "just one more" picture rather than see so many that none made as much of an impression as the fatigue such museum visits generated.

Q *Who said: "Grandpa has gone to Heaven and I'm sure God is finding him very useful"?*

A The six-year-old Princess Margaret Rose, upon learning of the death of George V.

Q *Who said the following about the appearance of Prince Charles at his investiture as Prince of Wales: "You could have put a suit of armor on that lad and sent him off to Agincourt!"?*

A The Mayor of Caernarvon at the time of the investiture at Caernarvon Castle in 1969.

Q *Which royal bridegroom said: "Absence will make the heart grow fonder," in explaining how he and his wife would deal with long separations caused by his naval career?*

A Prince Andrew, Duke of York.

Q *Who said: "I would rather not be in Gloucestershire, I think it's slightly overcrowded"?*

A Prince Andrew, commenting on where he and Fergie might eventually purchase a home. The county of Gloucestershire is called the "Royal Triangle" because Prince Charles, Princess Anne, and Prince Michael of Kent all have homes there.

Q *Who told Sarah Ferguson to "Buy your clothes for yourself, not for anybody else"?*

A Her husband, Prince Andrew. However, she says, "I dress for Andrew and only Andrew."

"Probably Ruin Her Day, Mate!"   When Prince Philip decided to become a pilot, he was put in the care of RAF Flight Lieutenant Caryl Gordon, who was set upon by superior officers intent on impressing the flight officer with the responsibility being given him. At the end of a lengthy discourse about care and safety, one officer looked directly into Gordon's eyes and left him with the concluding thought: "If you kill him, you realize what that will do to the Queen?" Philip is seen above after qualifying for his RAF wings in 1953.

—*British Information Services*

> **Funerals at Night** Until Queen Victoria left instructions ordering otherwise, all previous Kings and Queens had funerals held at night. She broke with that tradition and initiated the practice of lying-in-state for public viewing.

Q *Who said: "I am not the sort of woman who is going to meekly trot along behind. When I want to, I will stress a point"?*

A Sarah Ferguson, during an interview explaining how she saw her role as a royal wife.

Q *Who said: "Royalty is no excuse for bad manners"?*

A The Queen Mother to her daughters, a maxim Elizabeth II and Princess Margaret passed on to their children.

Q *Which royal has said more than once that the responsibilities of being royal outweigh the privileges?*

A Prince Andrew, who disdains the attention he receives when doing even the most ordinary things.

Q *Who said: "I have been trained never to show emotion in public"?*

A Queen Elizabeth II. The training reportedly came from her grandmother, Queen Mary.

Q *Who said: "My father was frightened of his mother. I was frightened of my father, and I'm damned well going to see to it that my children are frightened of me"?*

A King George V, who was successful in his wish.

Q *Who believes: "Ten minutes' doing is worth ten hours' watching"?*

A Prince Philip, who doesn't relish the role of spectator.

Q *What caused Winston Churchill to ask: "Is it the intention to wipe out the Royal Family in the shortest possible time?"*

A Winston Churchill said it upon learning that Prince Philip had flown a helicopter and intended to do so again with his wife and children. Years later both Prince Charles and Prince Andrew would become qualified Royal Navy pilots.

Q *Who said: "I will be good," upon learning she was to be the next monarch?*

A Queen Victoria.

Q Who was described as resembling a bell-hop because of his dress at Caenarvon Castle for the 1969 investiture of Charles, Prince of Wales?

A Antony Armstrong-Jones, Lord Snowdon, former husband of Princess Margaret Rose. He was dressed in a zippered green tunic, set off with a black silk cord belt, sans ceremonial sword. Prince Charles is seen in photo above immediately after the investiture.

—British Information Services

> **They're Not Alone**   There are no less than twenty-two other royal families who rule in various parts of the world. But by far and away the most public interest is generated by the British royal family.

Q *Who has said, more than once, the following about the gold plates used for state dinners at Buckingham Palace: "At least they don't break if you drop them"?*

A Prince Philip. The plates and other delicate pieces that are part of the banquet gold (about five tons in total) used during state dinners are moved between the kitchen and banquet hall in leather buckets.

Q *Who said: "It isn't everyone who gets married within a couple of months of being baptized"?*

A Prince Philip, who though originally baptized in the Greek Orthodox Church had to be re-baptized in the Church of England in order to marry Princess Elizabeth.

Q *Who said: "Life at Buckingham Palace isn't too bad, but too many formal dinners"?*

A Princess Diana in a letter to a friend.

Q *Which royal said: "We Princes are set as it were upon stages in the sight and view of all the world"?*

A Queen Elizabeth II, commenting on the royal lack of privacy.

Q *Who complained: "I have as much privacy as a goldfish in a bowl"?*

A Princess Margaret.

Q *Which monarch boasted: "Ours is not a family, it's a firm!"?*

A King George VI.

Q *Which royal thought: "What rot, and a waste of time, money, and energy all these state visits are"?*

A Edward VIII, who wrote the thoughts in his diary.

Q *Who said: "The trouble is that very often the worst people come first and the really nice people hang back because they don't want to be accused of sucking up"?*

A Prince Charles, describing his feelings about being introduced around during official functions.

Q Of whom was the following said: "Maybe he is interested in some subject, but it isn't a subject we teach here"?

A The comment appeared on a student report at Eton. The student being commented on was Antony Armstrong-Jones, who then went on to Jesus College, Cambridge, where he studied architecture. He became the Earl of Snowdon and Viscount Linley in October 1961, seventeen months after marrying Princess Margaret.

—British Information Services

Apology Accepted   The first worldwide tour Elizabeth II performed as Queen took six months to complete. During a review of African troops, a horse drawing the coach that carried the Queen and a ranking local official passed wind. Embarrassed, the Queen blurted a low "I'm sorry," to which the official shrugged and responded, "If you hadn't apologized, I would have thought it was the horse."

Q *Which royal posed the following to Winston Churchill: "How would you like to make a thousand speeches and never once be allowed to say what you think yourself?"*

A Edward VIII, later Duke of Windsor.

Q *Which royal asked the following question shortly after being married: "Am I divorced yet?"*

A Princess Anne, who was reacting to the large number of wedding stories which had appeared prior to her actual marriage.

Q *Identify the royal who advised a crowd they were getting too tight and too close with a humorous: "Please don't touch the exhibits"?*

A The Queen Mother.

Q *Which monarch said the following to his doctor as he prepared to knight him: "You used a knife on me. Now I'm going to use one on you"?*

A George VI. The doctor was his surgeon, James Learmonth.

Q *Which royal described Windsor Castle with these sad words: "Methinks I am in prison"?*

A Edward VI (1547–53) at age twelve, who added, "Here be no galleries, nor gardens to walk in!"

Q *Who said: "Be very, very careful of people who have tropical fish in their homes"?*

A Prince Philip, who added: "Such people are usually suffering from some psychiatric problem." He gave no explanation for this unusual opinion.

Q *Who said: "Don't forget that nowadays we have to compete with Elizabeth Taylor and the Beatles"?*

A Princess Alexandra.

Q *What did Queen Mary, Consort of George V (1910–36), describe as: "This dear glorious old castle so full of historical associations"?*

A The very same Windsor Castle Edward VI hated.

Q *George V said Sandringham was "the place I love better than anywhere in the world." How did his successor, Edward VIII, describe it?*

A "Dickens in a Cartier setting."

Q *Who described Princess Diana as: "A fashion disaster in her own right"?*

A Prudence Glynn, the fashion editor of *The Times* of London, in 1981. Her zing, however, was part of an article that appeared in *The International Herald Tribune*.

Q About which of Elizabeth II's sons was the following said by a schoolmaster at Gordonstoun: "If anyone tries to take the mickey out of him, he doesn't hesitate to fight back. He is just as good with verbalistics as he is with his fists"?

A Prince Andrew, who is seen here using his hand on the world's most famous mouse, Mickey, during a visit to Walt Disney World in Florida a few years ago.

—Walt Disney Company photo

Serious Business Under British law it is a major crime, punishable by death, to "violate" the reigning Queen or Queen Consort, or the wife of the Prince of Wales.

Q *Which royal called Balmoral "a pretty little castle in the old Scotch style"?*

A Queen Victoria.

Q *What did her son, Edward VII, call Balmoral?*

A "The Highland Barn of a thousand draughts." He also thought Buckingham Palace was "a sepulchre."

Q *What does Princess Margaret think of Buckingham Palace?*

A She calls it "a very cozy house." But George VI thought it "an icebox" and Edward VIII felt it had "a dank, musty smell."

Q *Which royal said: "Now I shall not go down like all the others," after learning how to use a handgun?*

A The Queen Mother, in 1940 during World War II.

Q *Who said the following to an aide wounded in an assassination attempt: "Be of good cheer, for you will never want. For the bullet was meant for me"?*

A Elizabeth I (1558–1603), who had been shot at while on her barge.

Q *Which royal said: "Life must go on," after being the target of six missed shots during Trooping of the Colour ceremonies?*

A Elizabeth II. The incident, by a seventeen year old who fired blanks, occurred in 1981.

Q *Which royal said: "We'll know in a moment if it's a bomb," after a loaded gun was thrown at him?*

A George V in 1935 to his son, the future George VI. The gun hit the King's horse but did not explode.

Q *Identify the royal who, after being stuck with a hatpin by a woman who attacked him, said such people "get no satisfaction from kicking the House of Parliament, whereas I am both handy and responsive"?*

A The Prince of Wales (future Edward VIII) in 1925.

Q *Name the royal who pleaded: "The poor creature is mad! Do not hurt her! She has not hurt me!"?*

A George III (1760–1820), after a woman attempted to stab him as he rode through the streets of London in his coach. She was immediately set upon by an angry crowd. The King himself was later thought mad and his son was named Regent.

Q Who said it was "Quite a feather in the family's cap" to have a relative marry into the royal family?

A The maternal grandmother of Lieutenant Mark Phillips of the Queen's Dragoon Guards, shortly after it was announced that he and Princess Anne were engaged in 1973. They are seen above in Munich, West Germany, a year earlier, where he was a member of Britain's Equestrian Team. He won an Olympic Gold Medal.

—British Information Services

> **Fact** Edward VII, who followed his mother Victoria to the throne, disliked the sound of jingling coins so much that all visitors had first to remove loose coins from their pockets.

Q *Who said: "Who are more important, three hundred spastics, or your own children?"*

A James Ogilvy, husband of Princess Alexandra, in 1971 while explaining the demands of public life: "If we don't see a lot more of our children we're going to pay the price . . . when they're older. You decide to spend an evening with the children but then someone . . . says, 'Please come to a film premier [and] help us raise another £1,500' [to] help, say, three hundred spastics.' "

Q *If Prince Charles visited your place of work, which three questions could you predictably expect him to ask you?*

A "What exactly are you doing? . . . Keep you busy, do they? . . . Pay you enough, do they?"

Q *Who confused George VI with Winston Churchill in telling Elizabeth II: "I'm so glad your father's been reelected!"?*

A The elderly mother of President Harry S. Truman, during Princess Elizabeth's 1951 Washington visit. She had just heard British election results on the radio.

Q *Who said: "He gave up his job, I gave up mine"?*

A Crisp, the personal valet of Edward VIII, who quit when his boss, having abdicated, asked him to move to France and continue working. Crisp was hired by George VI.

Q *Who proposed writing a letter to Adolf Hitler as "one ex-serviceman to another"?*

A George VI, in 1939. He was twice convinced not to by Prime Minister Neville Chamberlain, who felt he had secured "peace in our time."

Q *Who chastised a guest he considered incorrectly dressed by telling her: "I'm afraid you must have made a mistake. This is a dinner, not a tennis party"?*

A Edward VII (1901–10). The remark was made to the daughter of a Royal Navy admiral who appeared in a dress that had a hem fully an inch above her ankles.

Parley Bloody Vous?   Prince Philip has a low tolerance for people who bother him, namely, photographers, and he has been known to say, shout, and otherwise express his feelings toward them. Once a photographer could hardly believe what he lip-read Philip saying to him (through a car window) and demanded an explanation from a palace aide. "Prince Philip was speaking French," he was told by the straight-faced aide. The Duke of Edinburgh is seen here playing cricket in 1951 while in the Royal Navy.

—*British Information Services*

What the Butlers Did   On December 12, 1911, while George V and Queen Mary were in India greeting guests at the Durbar held in Delhi, Sir Harcourt Butler and Sir Montagu Butler were introduced by the officer serving as the king's local equerry with the simple "These are the two Butlers, sir." To which the king responded: "But what are their names?"

Q *Who exclaimed: "God be praised! The old harridan is dead!" when he was told his ex-wife had passed on?*

A Henry VIII (1509–47), who reportedly did not shed a tear at the death of his first wife of nearly twenty-four years, Catherine of Aragon, three years after their divorce.

Q *Which young Princess admonished a governess who ignored her for being naughty with: "You MUST answer. It's royalty speaking!"?*

A The future Elizabeth II. She later had an opportunity to herself hear royalty speaking when the Queen Mother learned of the incident.

Q *Who said: "His face at times wore such a look of beauty as might have lighted the face of a young knight who had caught a glimpse of the Holy Grail" in speaking about Edward VIII?*

A The Prime Minister at the time of the Abdication, Stanley Baldwin.

Q *On what is the following inscribed: "To the Prince of Wales from one who saw him conduct a blind beggar across the streets. In memory of a kind Christian action"?*

A A silver inkstand sent anonymously to Edward VII (1901–10).

Q *Who told the Prince of Wales in 1924: "You dress like a cad. You act like a cad. You are a cad. Get out!"*

A His father, George V, during a heated family discussion overheard by acquaintances of Prince Edward.

Q *Which royal said he felt "chained to the banqueting table"?*

A Edward, Prince of Wales (future Edward VIII).

Q *Who said: "It is sad to say, but I have no real job except that of being Prince of Wales"?*

A The future King Edward VIII, at age twenty-one, who held on to the job for twenty-five years.

Fact   Prince Charles once said, "If I wasn't who I am, I would love to have been a farmer." To satisfy that urge he once slipped away and worked on a farm milking cows, assisting at the birth of a calf, and generally trying his hand at various chores. He is seen in this 1970 photo fishing on the River Frome, near Wool, in Dorset.

—*British Information Services*

For Valor Britain's highest award for gallantry, the Victoria Cross, was created by Queen Victoria, who was tremendously moved by the heroism of British troops in the Crimean War. The first sixty-two medals, cast from captured Russian guns, were presented to veterans in May 1855.

Q *Which royal said: "We live above the shop," in describing the royal home/work environment?*

A Prince Philip.

Q *About which King did* The Times *of London say the following in an obituary: "Never was an individual less regretted by his fellow creatures"?*

A George IV (1820–30).

Q *Identify the head of state who sent a letter to Elizabeth II in which he called her his "Good and Big friend."*

A The Hon. Eduardo Montalva, president of Chile at the time (1968), in an invitation to visit his country.

Q *Who said: "Boy, the things I do for England!"?*

A Prince Charles, at a Gurkha training camp in the Far East as he was about to taste snake meat.

Q *Which royal thought schooling and education of common people should not be encouraged?*

A Queen Victoria. She believed that education would make them unfit to be "good servants and labourers."

Q *Whom did Queen Victoria consider a "half-mad firebrand"?*

A Prime Minister Gladstone.

Q *Who said the following about automobiles: "I'm told that they smell exceedingly nasty and are very shaky"?*

A Queen Victoria, who died without ever accepting an offer to ride in or drive one.

Q *Who once asked Prince Philip the following about snails: "How can you eat those beastly things?"*

A Elizabeth II, who also dislikes oysters, garlic, cigars, and tennis.

Q Which royal once compared the working press to a bunch of monkeys?

A Prince Philip, during a visit to Gibraltar. He studied the primates briefly, then glanced at the accompanying press corps and quipped: "Which are the monkeys?" Princess Anne is seen here during the 1954 trip offering a snack to the primates.

—British Information Services

The Press and the Prince "Royal-watching" has long been a favorite pastime of the English. Every member of the royal family is subjected to a seemingly endless stream of newspaper and magazine stories about even the most insignificant things they do. It reached full stride for Prince Charles during his first term at Cheam School, however, when no less than sixty-eight stories about him appeared in the press. Until he married Lady Diana years later and she would eclipse that figure time and again, this would remain the single greatest amount of coverage about one member of the family in so short a time.

Q *Which royal changed her dress after being asked by an aide: "What are you doing with that old black dress on you again?"*

A Queen Victoria. The question was posed by her servant, friend, and companion in widowhood, the Scotsman John Brown.

Q *Who thought Prince Philip's reading of a book instead of listening to the address being given at Prince Charles's confirmation was "bloody rude"?*

A The then Archbishop of Canterbury, Michael Ramsey.

Q *Who told Prince Philip: "At least I don't have a sister-in-law who is shacking up with a hippie"?*

A Elizabeth II's cousin by marriage, Angus Ogilvy. His wife, Princess Alexandra, is twenty-second in line to the throne. Philip had first told him, "You've landed us in it this time," which was a reference to Ogilvy having been linked to a scandal by the press. The caustic retort by Ogilvy alluded to the then much-publicized romance between Princess Margaret and Roddy Llewellyn.

Q *What did Queen Mary, wife of George V, say when formally introduced to a Coldstream Guard she previously had accidentally seen laying nude in his bunk?*

A She said what she could: "I believe we have met before."

Q *What remark by Prince Charles caused some of the leading shops on Savile Row to send letters of protest to Buckingham Palace?*

A His off-the-cuff statement: "I don't believe in fashion, full stop." Several designers and manufacturers contended the remark had the potential to wipe out decades of British leadership in men's fashions. Prince Charles, incidentally, buys his suits at Hawes & Curtis.

Q Which royal's lips were read on the balcony of Buckingham Palace and revealed: "I think I've got indigestion"?

A Elizabeth II, while standing and waving to the crowds with her newly married daughter Princess Anne. Balcony photo above is from the 1986 wedding of Prince Andrew and Sarah Ferguson, now the Duke and Duchess of York.

—*British Information Services*

> **Where There's a Will . . . No Way**   Traditionally royal wills are not made public, though speculation always takes place. It is usually fired by information obtained or leaked by someone close to the family.

Q *Which daughter of a President of the United States was described as "artificial and plastic" by Prince Charles?*

A Tricia Nixon. Both the British and American press had gone out of their way to connect the two young people romantically on a royal visit to the United States during the Nixon administration.

Q *Which royal considered the song "Alexander's Ragtime Band" "vulgar"?*

A Queen Mary, wife of George V. Her son, George VI, disliked opera so much he once hurled a book at someone who suggested the King should go more frequently, while her grandmother-in-law, Queen Victoria, considered Handel "tiresome."

Q *Who reacted to seeing an avocado for the first time by asking: "What in heaven's name is this?"*

A George V, who found it repulsive and refused to eat it.

Q *Who said: "It has been from people, rather than from textbooks, that I have got my education"?*

A Edward VIII.

Q *Who said: "I'm one of those stupid bums who never went to university . . . and it hasn't done me any harm"?*

A The Duke of Edinburgh, Prince Philip.

Q *What were his son Prince Charles's thoughts on the subject?*

A "I'm one of those stupid bums who went to university . . . well, I think it's helped me."

Q *Which royal said spending years in college or university was "a very much overrated pastime"?*

A Princess Anne.

Q *Which royal thought: "Rings on each finger improve an ugly hand"?*

A Queen Victoria, who considered her own hands unattractive and frequently wore several rings in public.

You're Welcome, Arf, Arf!   Elizabeth II made such a point of telling her children to always say "please" and "thank you" that young Prince Charles once told one of the Queen's Corgis to "Please fetch" a ball, and when the dog returned with it, the Prince said, "Thank you."

> **Fact** Royal children are taught at an early age exactly who they are. When he was hardly three years old, the future Prince of Wales corrected a member of the palace staff who had introduced him to an artist with a simple "This is Charles." Both the staff member and the artist, who had come to the palace to paint the child's portrait, were somewhat startled to hear a polite but firm young voice admonish: "This is *Prince* Charles." By his seventh birthday in 1955 the future Prince of Wales also displayed royal bearing.
>
> —*British Information Services*

Q *Which royal said the following about the Abdication of Edward VIII: "This is a pretty kettle of fish!"?*

A Queen Mary, mother of the abdicating King and widow of George V, to Prime Minister Stanley Baldwin, upon learning that her second oldest living son would now rise to the throne.

Q *Which monarch displayed his lack of knowledge about homosexuals with the quip: "I thought chaps like that shot themselves"?*

A George V, who in his younger days didn't seriously believe they existed and, as he got older, came to the conclusion that such people would surely take their own life once they discovered what they were.

Q *Identify the royal who once compared the working press to mosquitoes.*

A Prince Philip. This time during a trip to the Caribbean island of Dominica: "You have the mosquitoes, we have the press."

Q *Name the royal who calls the journalists that hound him "presstitutes."*

A Prince Andrew.

Q *Which royal complained: "I have been misrepresented and misreported since the age of seventeen"?*

A Princess Margaret Rose, who reportedly amended that afterwards to include her early years also.

Q *Name the royal who once said: "I treat the press as though they were children."*

A The former schoolteacher, Princess Diana.

Q *Which royal believes: "Strong winds blow germs away"?*

A The Queen Mother.

Q Who once told Queen Elizabeth II to: "Look after your Empire and I'll look after my life"?

A Her spunky sister, Margaret. They are seen above on board HMS *Vanguard*, the ship that took the royal family to South Africa while they were both still single. Margaret had flirted with a group of Royal Navy cadets and Elizabeth suggested such conduct was unbecoming a Princess.

—*British Information Services*

> **Royal Wit** While touring Admiral Horatio Nelson's historic ship HMS *Victory* in 1903, Edward VII was shown a bronze marker on the deck and told it was on the very spot where Nelson fell. With a straight face the King quickly replied, "I nearly tripped over the damn thing myself."

Q *Who made the following comment upon learning that World War II had begun: "More history for children to learn in a hundred years' time"?*

A The future Elizabeth II.

Q *Which royal described a near-fatal parachute plunge as "a rather hairy experience"?*

A Prince Charles, whose feet had become tangled in the lines during his first jump, in 1971.

Q *Which royal once gave an author a book inscribed: "From the humblest of writers to one of the greatest"?*

A Queen Victoria. The presentation was a copy of her book *More Leaves from a Journal of a Life in the Highlands* to Charles Dickens.

Q *Who said: "Up socks! Everything's going fine!" to Princess Margaret Rose just before she walked down the aisle to marry Antony Armstrong Jones?*

A Her brother-in-law, Prince Philip, who gave the bride away.

Q *What did Elizabeth II mouth to her brother-in-law, Lord Snowdon, when she noticed him smoking during the 1969 investiture of the Prince of Wales?*

A "Put that out, Tony!"

Q *Which royal was told: "The more we see of you the better," by a woman in his Court?*

A George IV (1820–30). The incident occurred in 1828, the first time he wore a kilt.

Q *Who told the future George VI: "Wait until I'm King . . . I'll chop your head off!"?*

A His brother, the future Edward VIII, when they had a disagreement as youngsters.

Sure, They Will   When Prince Edward, the future Edward VIII, first saw the clothes he was expected to wear at his investiture as Prince of Wales, he was horrified and called the costume a "preposterous rig." His mother, Queen Mary, told him: "Your friends [at school] will understand that as a Prince you are obliged to do certain things that may seem silly." Elizabeth II is seen above accompanying her son, Prince Charles, at the conclusion of his 1969 investiture as Prince of Wales.

—British Information Services

Oh, That Llewelyn!   When Prince Charles was preparing for his investiture as Prince of Wales in 1969, he was at times confronted by Welsh protesters carrying signs. On one occasion in London he approached a young couple with a sign and asked, "Who is Llewelyn?" And that's how he learned that Llewelyn (1246–82) had been the last Welsh-born Prince of Wales.

Q *Which royal once threatened to relocate to Australia?*

A Queen Victoria, during a particularly difficult period she was having early in her reign. "You will hear of me going with the children to live in Australia and to think of Europe as the Moon!" she said to her eldest daughter, Princess Victoria.

Q *Who said: "The children won't leave without me; I won't leave without the King; and the King will never leave"?*

A The Queen Mother, scoffing at speculation in the British press that the royal family was planning to take up residence in Canada for the duration of World War II.

Q *Name the song that caused George V to ask the Prince of Wales: "What's that damned tune you are whistling all the time?"*

A "A Pretty Girl Is Like a Melody," which the Prince had heard for the first time when he attended the Ziegfeld Follies during his 1919 tour that included the United States.

Q *Who said: "The Queen of England is to marry her horse-keeper, who has killed his wife to make room for her"?*

A Mary, Queen of Scots (1542–67). The comment referred to the Earl of Leicester, whose wife's death was termed accidental. The rumor of foul play was widespread and widely believed. However, the marriage didn't take place.

Q *Name the royal who was declared unfit as a subject for television interviews.*

A Captain Mark Phillips, husband of Princess Anne, who was described as "bloody hopeless" by professionals who were charged with preparing him to act, speak, and look good during television interviews.

Q *Which royal, at the conclusion of a dog sled ride in Canada, said: "That just slayed me."*

A Prince Charles. Pun intended.

Q Until George V had it removed, in which official document did the
following language appear: "The invocation or adoration of the
Virgin Mary or any other saint, and the Sacrifice of the Mass as
they are now used in the Church of Rome, are superstitious and
idolatrous"?

A The Parliamentary Declaration, used at the opening of Parliament.
George V, above, found the language to be severely anti-Catholic
and made it known he would not perform the ceremony unless it
was modified. Because of his changes, monarchs now need only
state that they are "a faithful Protestant."

—National Portrait Gallery

Aye, and Ye Wasted a Bullet, Too! After missing what he considered an easy shot while deer hunting, George V turned to his Scots hunting aide and bellowed: "Take this damned rifle away. Never let me see it again!" But the Scotsman snapped: "Yer Majesty, dinna waste yer breath damning the rifle. It was a verra bad shot!"

Q *Who said the following about Prince Philip: "Someone back home should tell the Prince it's about time he grew up"?*

A The Australian newspaper *Melbourne Herald* in an editorial that took him to task for what many Australians considered insulting remarks he made during his 1968 trip.

Q *Who said the following during a trip to Canada: "We don't come here for our health. We can think of better ways of enjoying ourselves"?*

A Prince Philip, in 1969. Some Canadians were so insulted that within the year the government replaced the likeness of Elizabeth II with former Canadian premiers on some of its money.

Q *Who said: "Work is the rent you pay for the room you occupy on Earth"?*

A The Queen Mother. It is one of her favorite expressions.

Q *Who said: "I did not realize that I could hate people as I do the Germans"?*

A Queen Mary, Consort to George V, in the early years of World War II shortly after the Battle of Britain had reached its peak.

Q *Who said: "You must not touch those toys. They are mine, I'm a Princess and you're not"?*

A The future Queen Victoria, then aged six, to a playmate.

Q *Who corrected a Lord who commented that the Queen had given birth to a very fine boy with: "A very fine PRINCE"?*

A Queen Victoria, in 1841 shortly after the birth of her first son (second child), the future Edward VII.

Q *Which royal called his own son "the greatest ass, liar and beast in the world"?*

A George II (1727–60), about Prince Frederick.

Q *Which monarch denied his daughter Princess Elizabeth's request for an education with the following logic: "To make women learned and foxes tame has the same effect ... to make them more cunning"?*

A James I and VI (1603–25). However, she married Frederick V, King of Bohemia, and as an adult learned to read books in several languages.

Q *Whom was General Charles de Gaulle speaking of when he said they were: "The only two people who have always shown me humanity and understanding"?*

A George VI and the Queen Mother. During the World War II years, De Gaulle often found Prime Minister Winston Churchill and other members of the government less than eager to treat him with the deference he thought he deserved.

Q *Who said: "I am just one among thousands of war widows"?*

A The Duchess of Kent in 1942, after her husband George, the brother of Edward VIII and George VI, was killed in a flying accident while on active duty in Scotland during World War II.

Q *Which royal called his father "a miserly martinet with an insatiable sexual appetite"?*

A Prince Frederick, talking about George II, who fathered at least one illegitimate child.

Q *Which monarch once blurted out the following about politicians in South Africa: "I would like to shoot them all!"?*

A George VI, on an official visit there in 1947 during which he became frustrated with the attitudes and political undercurrents. The Queen Mother, knowing his moods, replied: "But, dear, you couldn't shoot them ALL."

Interrupt Whenever You Wish, My Boy!   When the Duke of Windsor was young, he once tried to interrupt a conversation Edward VII was having with others over lunch. He was promptly told to mind his manners and wait for permission to speak. Finally Edward VII turned to the fidgeting youth and indicated he might speak. "It's too late now, Grandpa," came the reply. "It was a caterpillar on your lettuce . . . but you've eaten it."

Lucky Seven Times Seven assassination attempts were made on the life of Queen Victoria. In five of the attempts, the would-be assassins had failed to load their guns.

Q *Who said: "I am nothing more than a sailor like yourselves"?*

A The future William IV (1830–37), while still Prince of Wales, at the time of his first shipboard naval duty in the late 1700s.

Q *Which Consort once instructed a governess to whack or spank a Princess every now and then, "For the cursed bastard she is."*

A Anne Boleyn, second wife of Henry VIII, who despised the daughter of Catherine of Aragon, Princess Mary (future Mary I, 1553–58). Anne was beheaded in 1536.

Q *Who called entertainer Tom Jones a "bloody awful singer"?*

A Prince Philip, during a question-and-answer session after a speech the day after he had heard Jones perform. When Jones was told of the remark, he responded: "I was singing for charity, not auditioning for Prince Philip."

Q *During a visit to a South American dictatorship, which royal exclaimed: "It's a pleasant change to be in a country that isn't ruled by its people."*

A Prince Philip, to Paraguaian strongman Alfredo Stroessner in 1969.

Q *Identify the monarch who stepped before microphones he thought were out of order and said: "The damned things aren't working!"?*

A George VI. They were working and his remarks were carried.

Q *Who said the following in June 1937: "What a damnable wedding present"?*

A The Duke of Windsor (former Edward VIII), upon receiving a letter from his brother George VI saying that the Duchess of Windsor could not be legally called "Her Royal Highness." The prohibition also extended to any children the couple might have. (Though this quote has been popularly accepted as fact, Sir Walter Monckton, who personally received the letter from George VI and delivered it to the Duke, insisted the Duke had said sarcastically: "This is a nice wedding present!"—almost the exact words George VI had used as Monckton was departing.)

Our Mistake, Madam Charles II (1649–85) frequently had more than one mistress at the same time. At one point when both Protestant Nell Gwynne and Catholic Louise-Renée de Kéroualle, above, held the King's attention, Nell was surprised to have her coach attacked by Londoners throwing fruit. "Stop it, you fools! I'm the Protestant whore, not the Catholic one!" she shouted. (Another version of this quote has her saying: "Pray, good people, desist, I am the Protestant whore!")

—Talbot Collection

> **A Lead Rabbit's Foot?** Edward VII frequently carried a spent bullet in his pocket for good luck. It had been fired at him by an assassin in Brussels the year before he came to the throne.

Q *Which royal commented that Niagara Falls "looked very damp"?*
A Elizabeth II. No pun intended.

Q *Which King said the following about his ancestors: "A strange busload to be traveling through eternity together"?*
A George V (1910–36).

Q *Which future Queen commented after the birth of a Princess: "Now there will be four bears instead of three"?*
A The young Princess Elizabeth (future Elizabeth II), upon being told that she had a new sister. One of her favorite family games was crawling around with her parents and growling like a bear.

Q *Which monarch told a Prince of Wales to take every opportunity "to relieve yourself"?*
A George V, to his son, the future Edward VIII, suggesting that such opportunities could prevent discomfort when obliged to sit through long speeches.

Q *Which royal said: "The art world thinks of me as an uncultured polo-playing clod"?*
A Prince Philip.

Q *Who said: "I know I'm rude . . . but it's fun"?*
A Prince Philip in 1963, who continues having "fun" and giving the press a field day.

Q *Which royal once admitted sometimes thinking, "I wish I hadn't said that"?*
A Prince Philip, commenting some years ago on how it felt to read his often abrasive remarks in the press.

Q *Name the King who said: "I'll pull down my breeches and they shall also see my arse!"*
A James I and VI (1567–1625), responding to a suggestion that pushing crowds only wanted to get closer for a better look at His Majesty.

Royal Triskaidekaphobia   Queen Elizabeth II is among the thousands of people who have a strong fear or dislike of the number 13, clinically known as triskaidekaphobia. Once when a dinner for twelve was scheduled at Buckingham Palace and Prince Charles showed up unexpectedly, the Queen ordered that two tables be used, thereby creating two smaller groups. Palace staffers used a large tablecloth arranged to conceal the separation.

—British Information Services

Royal Potpourri

Four and twenty Yankees, feeling very dry,
Went across the border to get a drink of rye.
When the rye was opened, the Yanks began to sing
"God bless America, but God save the King!"
—*Prohibition era ditty which*
amused the future Edward VIII

Q *Name the future monarch who was determined to cross Niagara Falls in a wheelbarrow pushed by a tightrope walker.*

A The flamboyant Edward VII (1901–10), who as the nineteen-year-old Prince of Wales in 1860 was only dissuaded from participating in the dangerous stunt by hysterical aides. The invitation had been extended by tightrope walker Charles Blondin during Edward's visit to America.

Q *Which royal once removed his swimtrunks in the water off Barbados and waved them at onlookers?*

A The 1983 exhibition was by Prince Andrew.

Q *Name the royal who reportedly had three breasts.*

A The second wife of Henry VIII, Anne Boleyn, whom he had beheaded in 1536 after three years of marriage.

Q *Name the former male royal employee who underwent an operation to become a female.*

A David Payne, who had worked for Princess Margaret as a footman. His sex was changed during an operation in France in 1969.

Telephobia   Queen Mary, wife of George V, had such an aversion to telephones she once gave fancy telephone covers to several friends as Christmas gifts. The Queen considered phones "absolutely awful devices" that shouldn't be seen in a proper home.

Royal Performances   Princess Margaret, seen in this 1969 portrait by the Earl of Snowdon, has always had a flair for show business, and musical comedies in particular. Friends say her impersonations of Sophie Tucker and Ethel Merman are first-rate. So infectious is her stage presence when entertaining the rest of the family at parties that it takes little effort to convince the Queen to join her in a duet of stage show songs.

—British Information Services

> **Fact**   Until 1968, it was prohibited by English law for any actor or actress to portray a living member of the royal family. The first member so portrayed after the ban was Elizabeth, the Queen Mother, in the 1972 stage production of *Crown Matrimonial* at the Haymarket Theatre. She was depicted as the Duchess of York during the 1936 Abdication crisis.

Q *What is the favorite party game of the royal family?*
A Charades, for which they employ a wide selection of costumes.

Q *Which royal is considered to have the best ability to mimic accents?*
A Elizabeth II, who only does them at gatherings of family members and very close friends. Her American and Cockney are reported to be knee-slappers.

Q *Name the first monarch to be recorded on film.*
A Queen Victoria, during her Diamond Jubilee ceremonies in 1897.

Q *Which Princess played Queen Victoria in a Peter Sellers movie?*
A Princess Margaret. The 1964 private production was a professional effort, not a home movie. However, it was never intended for public release.

Q *Name the Prince who played a Prince in a legitimate theater production.*
A Edward, Prince of Wales (future Edward VII), in 1882, when he was forty-two years old. He persuaded a Paris producer to let him do a guest appearance with Sarah Bernhardt in *Fedora*. Edward played a dead Prince.

Q *Identify the subject of a proposed movie that caused Queen Elizabeth II to react with unusual frankness and term the suggestion disgusting and "obnoxious."*
A An ill-conceived project in the mid-1970s that would have put "the sex life" of Jesus Christ on the screen.

> **The Keystone King?**   George VI was an avid home movie fan who frequently had an uproarious time entertaining close friends and members of the family by having such movies played backwards.

How About Cowboys Who Kiss Their Horses?   George V found movies with romantic scenes rather boring and would often vent his displeasure by directing witty and caustic remarks at the theater screen. He preferred both silent movies and "talkies" with action and adventure.

Royal Singing Debut   Prince Charles made his London singing debut in 1985 with the Bach Choir at Royal Albert Hall on the 300th anniversary of Johann Sebastian Bach's birth. The choir, which Prince Charles is president of, performed the Mass in B Minor for an audience of 5,000

—British Information Services

> **Slower, Slower . . . Faster, Faster** George V so revered the National Anthem, "God Save the King," that it was common knowledge among musicians that the King wished it played at a very slow, dignified tempo and any performance to the contrary would be met with royal displeasure. However, his son, Edward VIII, often became annoyed with musicians who dragged it out, and more than once let it be known he wanted the tempo speeded up considerably. (After he abdicated and returned to Britain as the Duke of Windsor, he admitted to a slight discomfort when he was greeted by a band playing the shorter version . . . the full anthem is only played for the reigning monarch.)

Q *Name the royal who was cast as the baby Jesus in a family Christmas play.*

A Princess Margaret, in 1940.

Q *Which royal invited the first Royal Command Performance of a motion picture film?*

A Edward, Prince of Wales (future Edward VII), on July 21, 1896. The previous month cinematographer Birt Acres had made a film of Edward and the Princess of Wales attending the Cardiff Exhibition and asked for permission to exhibit it publicly. Before agreeing, Edward commanded Acres to show it to him (and forty guests) at Marlborough House. In addition to this film, Acres also showed twenty other shorts.

Q *Who was the first reigning monarch to invite a Royal Command Performance of a motion picture?*

A Queen Victoria, on November 23, 1897, when she was seventy-eight years old. Films made during her Diamond Jubilee were shown by the Lumière Cinématographe company at Windsor Castle. A full orchestra conducted by Leopold Wenzel provided background music.

Q *Who requested the first Royal Command Performance of a non-documentary, nonhistorical, or non-news feature film?*

A Queen Alexandra, widow of Edward VII, on August 4, 1916, when she was seventy-two years old. The film, *Comin' Through the Rye*, was shown at Marlborough House.

Q *Who were the first King and Queen to ask for a Royal Command Performance of an acted feature film?*

A George V and Queen Mary, on February 27, 1917, at Buckingham Palace. The film was *Tom Brown's Schooldays*.

The Gunfight at Buckingham Corral?   The Queen Mother is probably among a handful of Britons who knows *The Shooting of Dan McGrew* verbatim and will recite it with little encouragement. However, during a 1984 visit to London, another devotee of the poem, President Ronald Reagan, became involved in a friendly verbal duel with her to see who knew it best. In photo above, she is seen attending the opening of Queen Mother Hall at Westfield College, University of London, in 1982.

—*British Information Services*

> **Fact** Charles II (1660–85) believed the powdered remains of Egyptian pharoahs transmitted "ancient greatness" to his person when he rubbed the mummy dust over his body.

Q *Name the first reigning monarch to ask for a Royal Command Performance at a public movie theater.*

A George VI, on November 1, 1946, at the Empire Theatre in London. The King, and his family, saw David Niven in *A Matter of Life and Death.*

Q *Who was the first royal to appear on television?*

A Princess Marina, Duchess of Kent, whose husband had two brothers who would become King and herself became the aunt of Elizabeth II. Her image was transmitted during an experiment in 1935.

Q *Identify the first reigning monarch to appear live on television.*

A George VI, on May 12, 1937, when part of his coronation was broadcast to the approximately 2,000 television sets believed to exist at the time in Britain.

Q *What year did Elizabeth II make the first live Christmas television broadcast?*

A In 1957. It was broadcast throughout the Commonwealth.

Q *Who was the first royal to consent to a television interview?*

A Prince Philip, who appeared on the BBC on May 29, 1961, in a weekly news-interview format show called *Panorama.*

Q *Who was the first monarch to own a television set?*

A Edward VIII.

Q *Identify the two royals who have appeared in school productions of* Macbeth.

A Prince Philip and Prince Charles. Both appeared in Gordonstoun efforts, years apart, with the father playing Donalbain and the son in the title role of the Scots king. Charles also played a king in *The Pirates of Penzance.*

Q *Who was Prime Minister when Edward VIII abdicated in 1936?*

A Stanley Baldwin.

Q *Which royal reportedly enjoyed the Beatles' movie* Yellow Submarine *so much she has seen it (at last count) five times?*

A Elizabeth II.

Elizabeth II Launches First Nuclear Sub   In 1960, on the 155th anniversary of Nelson's victory in the Battle of Trafalgar, Queen Elizabeth II pulled down the lever of a ship's telegraph to launch Britain's first nuclear-powered submarine, HMS *Dreadnought.* Prince Philip, in naval uniform, looks on.

—British Information Services

Sentimental Flag George VI asked for the last flag that flew over the British Residency in Lucknow, India, when that country was proclaimed independent in 1947. He had it flown over Windsor Castle.

Q *What do the following actresses have in common: Pamela Stephenson, Suzanne Danielle, and Eve Lohman?*

A All have played Princess Diana in television productions. (Ms. Stephenson has also played Queen Elizabeth II.)

Q *Name the luxury cruiseship launched by Princess Diana on November 15, 1984.*

A The P & O Lines' *Royal Princess.*

Q *Who was the first King to travel in a submarine?*

A James I and VI (1567–1625), who made an underwater passage from Westminster to Greenwich in 1615 in a wooden boat covered in impermeable leather. It had been proposed by English mathematician William Bourne and built by Cornelius Van Drebbel.

Q *Name the ship that George VI and Queen Mary crossed the Atlantic on in May 1939.*

A The liner *Empress of Australia.* Because of the tension in Europe at the time (only four months before the outbreak of World War II), there was considerable concern for the safety of the royal couple, including speculation of a potential attack by German U-boats. But the trip, which included a visit to the United States, was uneventful.

Q *Identify the yacht that the Prince of Wales and Wallis Simpson cruised aboard in 1930.*

A *Rosaura,* followed by a visit to Switzerland.

Q *Which royal can still claim, if desired, the carcasses of all porpoises and whales discovered on Cornish beaches?*

A Prince Charles, who may also claim the cargo of Cornish shipwrecks.

Q *Name the Royal Navy aircraft carrier that Prince Andrew served on during the Falkland Islands war in 1982.*

A HMS *Invincible.* He served as a helicopter pilot and remained on board for several months after the war. His commission in the Royal Navy is twelve years.

Q *Identify the first female member of the royal family to visit a hairdresser's establishment instead of having them summoned to the royal household.*

A Princess Elizabeth, when she was in Malta where her husband was stationed while in the Royal Navy.

The Original   Princess Diana, seen here visiting handicapped children in Greater Manchester, is credited with causing hairdressers to duplicate her hairstyle for more women than any other style since Jacqueline Kennedy's much-copied style of the early 1960s. Diana's cut has reportedly been done twice as many times already.

—*British Information Services*

Only Her Hairdresser Knows for Sure Diana-watchers report that Kevin of "Headlines" beauty salon is called upon to do her hair three or more times each week.

Q *Name the two royal yachts used by Queen Victoria.*
A One was *Fairy* and the other was *Victoria and Albert*.

Q *Identify the King credited with bringing order to maritime navigation.*
A Henry VIII, who formally established Trinity House in 1514. It still continues, more than 473 years later, to provide essential aids to navigation.

Q *Name the future King who devised one of the earliest known sets of naval signals (semaphore) for ship-to-shore communication.*
A James II (1685–88), while he was Lord High Admiral of the British Fleet.

Q *Identify the King recognized for changing the complexion of the Navy from armed merchant ships to man-of-war fighting vessels.*
A Henry VIII, who understood the importance of both cannon and sailing ships and in the early sixteenth century financed a new navy with money taken from the Church.

Q *Identify the monarch who did a commercial advertising endorsement for a piano company.*
A Edward VII, in 1910. The product was the Angelus Player Piano.

Q *Name the royal who ordered nearly 30,000 black mulberry trees planted as an incentive to silkworms to produce more silk.*
A James I and VI (1567–1625), who had been misinformed. Silk-producing worms eat the leaves of white, not black, mulberry trees.

Q *Name the first monarch to cross the Atlantic by air.*
A Elizabeth II, who had also done it as a Princess in 1951.

Q *Identify the first monarch to travel around the world.*
A Elizabeth II, who is without a doubt the most traveled of all British sovereigns.

Mary Jane and the King   James I and VI (1567–1625) ordered that each of the Jamestown (America) colonists be given plots of land for the planting of hemp (marijuana) and flax cultivation in 1611. These grants were reported to be the first privately owned properties in the colony. By 1619 the Virginia General Assembly ordered that all who had hemp seed must plant it in the following season, legislating what amounted to the first marijuana law in America.

Q The Royal Academy has portraits of all the Kings and Queens of England dating back to what year?

A The collection, which contains works by Holbein, Van Dyck, Rubens, and other masters, includes portraits of all England's monarchs from A.D. 653 to the present. Queen Elizabeth II is seen here during a 1953 exhibit studying a Winterhalter painting of the Royal Family in 1846.

—British Information Services

PRINCESS DIANA'S FAMOUS ANCESTORS

Diana, Princess of Wales, can count some of history's most famous—
and in a few cases infamous—names in her ancestral family tree. Below
is a partial list:

England's Lord Protector Oliver
   Cromwell
English Prime Minister Winston S.
   Churchill
U.S. President George Washington
U.S. President John Adams
U.S. President John Quincy Adams
U.S. President Theodore Roosevelt
U.S. President Franklin D. Roosevelt
U.S. President Calvin Coolidge
French Prime Minister Giscard
   D'Estaing
Spain's King Juan Carlos
Russian Empress Catherine the Great
German Chancellor Otto von Bismarck
Nazi Reichsmarshal Herman Goering
General George S. Patton
Author Johann Wolfgang Goethe

Author Louisa May Alcott
Author Virginia Woolf
Author Graham Greene
Author George Orwell
Author Harriet Beecher Stowe
Author Ralph Waldo Emerson
Author Erle Stanley Gardner
Author George Sand
Actor Humphrey Bogart
Actor Orson Welles
Actress Olivia de Havilland
Actress Lillian Gish
Actress Lee Remick
Millionaire Gloria Vanderbilt
Millionaire Nelson Bunker Hunt
Lawrence of Arabia
The Marquis de Sade
The Aga Khan

Q *Besides their names what did George II, George IV, and George VI
have in common?*

A They were all left-handed.

Q *What was the reason for Prince Charles's visit to Boston in September 1986?*

A To make the keynote speech at Harvard University's 350th anniversary. The Prince is a graduate of England's Cambridge University, as
was John Harvard, founder and namesake of the American institution.
It was Charles's eighth visit to the United States in fifteen years but
his first ever to Boston.

Q *When did the first reigning monarch decide to make a radio broadcast?*

A On April 23, 1924, George V chose to commemorate the opening of
the Empire Exposition at Wembley. Because of a relay system of
loudspeakers which carried the broadcast to gathered crowds in cities
and towns throughout England, it was estimated that 10 million heard
the king's voice for the first time.

Queen Time Elizabeth, the Queen Mother, seen in this 1950 photo, has a well-known reputation for tardiness which is the absolute opposite of her daughter, Elizabeth II, to whom punctuality is almost a virtue. To keep peace in the palace, Elizabeth II's aides usually advise the Queen Mother's secretary that functions are starting a half-hour sooner than they actually are.

—British Information Services

Wake up Beauty Call   The late Duchess of Windsor reportedly underwent a daily early morning makeup application for several years by an expert from the fashionable Elizabeth Arden cosmetics concern in Paris. During the World War II years the company also produced black face cream used by Allied soldiers on night missions.

Q *Name the King who kept the clocks at Sandringham running one half hour fast in order to ensure that he and members of the royal family would always be on time for appointments.*

A George V. On the night he died, his son and heir, Edward VIII, had them all reset correctly, undoing twenty-five years of tradition.

Q *What tell-tale sign has come to be taken as a warning by palace staffers that Queen Elizabeth II has become impatient with somebody or something?*

A The reflex habit of turning her engagement ring around her finger several times usually indicates she is displeased.

Q *Which royal was trained as a Cordon Bleu cook?*

A Princess Diana, who enjoys cooking for her husband.

Q *Which royal worked as a volunteer cook in a Red Cross canteen during World War II?*

A The Duchess of Windsor, in the Bahamas.

Q *Where does the butter served in Buckingham Palace come from?*

A The Royal Dairy at Windsor Castle. It is appropriately stamped with a small crown.

Q *Why does Elizabeth II smile and let someone else open cans marked "Mixed Nuts"?*

A Because Prince Philip once gave her a can so marked from which a "snake" jumped out.

Q *Who was the first monarch to be called "Your Majesty"?*

A Henry VIII, Prince of Wales, Duke of York, and King of Ireland (1509–47).

Q *Which King was called "the Lion of Justice"?*

A Henry I (1100–35).

Q *Which royal said: "I was that damned fool," when told "some damned fool" had paid over $1,500 for a single stamp?*

A George V, an avid stamp collector. The newspaper report had been brought to the King's attention by his friend Sir Arthur Davidson.

Q Who began the collecting which eventually became the Royal Stamp Collection?

A Queen Elizabeth II's grandfather, King George V. She is seen here looking through one of the volumes of the priceless collection in 1961.

—British Information Services

Fact Shortly after the death of George V in 1936, artisans at the British Royal Mint began preparing dies for coins with the likeness of Edward VIII, according to tradition, facing right. However, Edward felt that the left side of his face was his best, so designers were ordered to transfer those features to the coin (which would still be facing right!). Nonetheless, the man who would be King for less than one year was unhappy with the results and insisted that the coins be struck with his likeness facing left. Unable to start all over again in the short time left before the dies were due, mint officials employed a process whereby an electrotype of the rejected likeness was attached to a machine usually used to cut new steel dies. By setting the machine so that both the electroplate and the cutter moved in *reverse*, they were able to produce a likeness of Edward VIII facing left . . . which he approved, not noticing that his hair was parted now on the wrong side.

"Confusability" Considered When Britain prepared for conversion to decimal-value postage stamps, the Applied Psychology Research Unit at Cambridge was commissioned to conduct extensive tests on twenty-five colors to avoid "confusability." Since a likeness of the reigning monarch appears on British stamps (in this case, Arnold Machin's profile of Elizabeth II), there was concern that the combination of the new decimal values and similar colors on stamps could cause problems. "Decimalisation Day" was February 15, 1971, and within eighteen months all other stamps issued since 1911 were declared invalid for postage. The two exceptions were the £1 Queen Elizabeth II and £1 Windsor Castle stamps, which were adopted into the decimal range.

—British Information Services

Proclamation of Accession   In addition to numerous readings throughout the British Isles and Commonwealth, the Proclamation of Accession, to signify a new reign, is read at three different locations near Windsor Castle: Castle Hill; Henry VIII Gateway; and the Eton side of Windsor Bridge. On February 8, 1952, the Mayor of Windsor did the Castle Hill reading at the statue of Queen Victoria. Note that the embroidered Royal Cypher on the uniform of the Heralds was still "G.R." (Georgius Rex) rather than the "E.R." of his daughter.

—British Information Services

Second-Hand Statue The horseback statue, in Yorkshire, of Charles II (1660–85) that depicts the King trampling Oliver Cromwell was originally commissioned for Poland. It was to signify the King of Poland trampling a Turkish invader, but when the time came to pay, the Poles balked. By making some slight changes, the sculptor was able to sell it to England as "Charles II Conquering Cromwell." Monument buffs point out, however, that Cromwell is wearing a turban.

Q *Name the two British monarchs whose likenesses have appeared on more coins than any others.*

A Queens Victoria, whose reign (1837–1901) was the longest, and Elizabeth II, who ranks as the tenth longest to date but has been Queen during the years of greatest coinage. All British coins carry likenesses of the reigning monarch.

Q *Identify the first English monarch whose likeness was struck on a coin.*

A Alfred the Great (871–c. 899), who ordered that pennies be struck in 886. He was "King of all England." That was the start of an 1,100-year uninterrupted minting of coins by what has become known as the British Royal Mint.

Q *On what day does Elizabeth II distribute silver coins to a number of people equal to twice her age?*

A Maundy Thursday, three days before Easter. The ancient tradition of giving alms to the elderly or poor had not been practiced by a sovereign for nearly 250 years until it was again begun by Elizabeth's grandfather, George V.

Q *Identify the royal whom Assistant Secretary of the Navy Franklin D. Roosevelt escorted on a tour of the U.S. Naval Academy at Annapolis in 1919.*

A The Prince of Wales, future Edward VIII, and later Duke of Windsor. During the same trip Edward visited the U.S. Military Academy at West Point and was escorted around by the Superintendent, General Douglas MacArthur.

Q *Where was the future Edward VIII when he got his first view of New York City?*

A On a pier in Jersey City, New Jersey. He had arrived from Washington, D.C., by train during his 1919 tour.

Q *Name the royal who popularized use of the handkerchief.*

A Richard, Prince of Wales (future Richard II, 1377–99). Some historians credit him with inventing it.

Q Prior to Queen Elizabeth II's July 1958 trip into an underground mine, when had a British monarch last journeyed below?

A Not since her grandfather, King George V, visited a mine in 1912. She is seen here at Rothes Colliery, Kirkcaldy, Scotland, before descending 1,600 feet and spending forty minutes watching the full coal-mining cycle.

—British Information Services

Crocodile Tears?   During her 1961 visit to Gambia, Elizabeth II was presented with a young crocodile as a gift for Prince Andrew. Her private secretary, Sir Martin Charters, had the honor of housing the animal in his bathtub for the remainder of the trip and reportedly accepted the hospitality of others in the royal party who offered use of their facilities when needed.

Q *Name the first member of the royal family to attend an organized public Soccer League game.*

A Edward, Prince of Wales (future Edward VII), on March 20, 1886.

Q *Identify the first royal to ride a bicycle (actually it was a quadricycle).*

A Prince Albert, Consort to Queen Victoria, who first rode one in 1851.

Q *Which sovereign flatly refused to knight admitted or proven homosexuals?*

A George V.

Q *Name the first reigning British sovereign to visit China.*

A Elizabeth II, in October 1986.

Q *Identify the royal who acquired a firefighter's uniform so he could watch fires from close by without attracting attention.*

A Edward, Prince of Wales (future Edward VII).

Q *Which royal found actually visiting the Sphinx in Egypt very disappointing?*

A Queen Mary, Consort of George V. Exactly what she expected is not known.

Q *How did Queen Victoria feel about giving women the right to vote?*

A She was outspokenly against it.

Q *Which sovereign told a Prime Minister not to trust the Russians?*

A Queen Victoria. The Prime Minister was Disraeli.

Q *Which royal was very outspoken in his distrust of people who didn't believe in God?*

A Edward, Prince of Wales (future Edward VII).

Q Of all the things she saw during her "supermarket stop" while on the royal visit to the United States in October 1957, what item was of particular interest to the Queen?

A Shopping baskets (carts) on wheels that had a seat for toddlers. The Queen is seen here talking to a mother in the Washington, D.C., self-service supermarket where she and Prince Philip spent fifteen minutes talking to the staff and customers.

—British Information Services

Fish or Cut Bait   Elizabeth I (1558–1603) was so intrigued with the thought of gathering vast wealth that she was often easy prey for adventurers proffering ambitious or wild schemes. One such was the alchemist Lannoy, who persuaded the Queen to finance his experiments to change base metal into gold. After several unsuccessful attempts, combined with what the Queen considered transparent excuses, she lost patience and faith in his ability and had him confined to the Tower of London.

Q *Identify the Prince who enjoyed having winter house guests, and friends who visited, stand still while he threw snowballs at them.*

A Edward, Prince of Wales (future Edward VII). He was frequently joined in such target practice by his five children.

Q *Which monarch collected old snuff boxes?*

A Edward VIII.

Q *Identify the female member of the royal family who has brought down a rhinoceros with a big-game rifle and can play bongo drums.*

A No, it isn't Princesses Margaret or Anne. Would you believe the Queen Mother?

Q *Who was the first member of the royal family to make a radio broadcast?*

A Edward, Prince of Wales (future Edward VIII), on October 7, 1922, from York House. He made an address to British Boy Scouts unable to attend a national rally being held at Alexandra Palace.

Q *Which King, because he spoke no English, communicated with his ministers in French?*

A The German-born George I (1714–27). The Norman Kings did so as well, since that was the lingua franca of the Court.

Q *Who was the last English King to lead his troops into battle?*

A George II (1727–60), who reportedly organized each day of the Battle of Dettingen in 1743 with the precision of a drill sergeant.

Q *Which future King functioned as Regent (or sovereign de facto) for nine years before following his father to the throne?*

A George IV (1820–30). He was named Regent on February 5, 1811, when George III (1760–1820) was declared insane.

Q *Which Princess includes the rock group Abba and Tchaikovsky among her favorite music?*

A Diana, Princess of Wales.

Q *Identify the "three B's" that Prince Charles ranks as among his favorite musicians.*

A Bach, Beethoven, and the Beatles.

Q Name the horse owned by Queen Elizabeth II that in 1957 gave her third winner in a row in the 2,000 Guineas Trial Stakes at Kempton Park.

A In 1955 she won with Alexander; in 1956 it was High Veldt; and the horse that produced the "hat trick" in 1957 was the colt Doutelle. She is seen here in the winner's enclosure accompanied by her trainer, Captain C. Boyd Rochfort.

—British Information Services

Q Name the traditional ceremony that honors the birthday of Elizabeth II.

A The Trooping of the Colour. On June 15, 1970, it was the turn of the 2nd Battalion, Scots Guards, to have their Colour trooped. In this photo, the Queen is riding Burmese, a black mare presented to her by the Canadian Royal Mounted Police.

—British Information Services

Dog and Horse Go Down in History   When E. Carter Preston was commissioned to design a new seal for the ancient county of Lancaster, England, in 1954, he suggested that perhaps Queen Elizabeth II would be delighted to have one of her pet dogs included in the device. He guessed correctly, and she provided him with photos of Susan, her Corgi, and Winston, the police horse she rode at the time for ceremonial occasions. The Corgi can be seen near the horse's front feet.

—*British Information Services*

> **Q** Who redesigned the Great Seal of England to mark the reign of
> Queen Elizabeth II?
>
> **A** Gilbert Ledward, in 1953. The obverse (top) shows the Queen
> mounted and wearing the uniform of Colonel-in-Chief of the Gren-
> adier Guards. The inscription is the Latin form of the full Royal
> Style and Title. The reverse shows her throned and robed, with the
> Sceptre in her right hand and the Orb in her left. Correctly called
> the Great Seal of the Realm, it changes with each new reign and
> is only used on certain state documents.
>
> —*British Information Services*

Voiding the Seal   Shortly after rising to the throne, new sovereigns traditionally void the seal of the former ruler by striking it with a heavy hammer.

Q *Name the famous relation of Princess Diana who refused an invitation from Elizabeth II to be knighted.*

A Author Graham Greene, who directed his secretary to decline in "the normal way."

No Test Needed   Princess Anne and her husband, Captain Mark Phillips, are seen above wearing team outfits as they prepared to leave England for the 1976 Olympic Games in Montreal. Anne was the only female competitor who was exempted from taking a sex test.

—British Information Services

How to Write a Best-Seller Shortly after he became King, Edward VII learned that the wife of a former tenant farmer at Sandringham had written a book which mentioned he permitted game animals to have virtual run of the property so he and his friends would have an easy job when they came hunting. She noted, in detail, how these animals ate and destroyed the meager crops her family grew. So outraged was Edward that he briefly forgot she no longer lived on the estate, and ordered her evicted. That being denied to him, he then ordered that all copies of the book be bought and destroyed.

Q *Who was the first Queen to have a book dedicated to her?*

A Elizabeth I. The book, by Dr. Timothy Bright, was about what would later be called stenographic.

Q *Which British monarch did author Truman Capote once say he would like to have been in a past incarnation?*

A Henry VIII. Capote also said he would have liked to have been the Roman emperor Caligula; Catherine the Great of Russia; Cleopatra; and Joseph Stalin, among others.

Q *Which royal wrote the introduction to the best-selling book* Captains and Kings?

A Prince Charles, who has written no less than eight other introductions and two books himself.

Q *Identify the royal whose photographs have been published as a book titled* Birds from Britannia.

A Prince Philip, who has also displayed talent as a painter.

Q *Name the only monarch to date to have written an autobiography.*

A Edward VIII, who penned *A King's Story*.

Q *Identify the monarch who ordered the first Bibles printed in the vernacular.*

A James I (1603–25).

Q *Who once gave Elizabeth, the Queen Mother, a secondhand book of poetry as a Christmas gift because it was all he could afford at the time?*

A The young Royal Navy officer who would shortly marry her daughter, Prince Philip.

Girl Guides at Windsor Miss Violet Synge was captain of the Girl Guides company formed at Windsor during the World War II years so that Princesses Elizabeth and Margaret could experience camping and related activities so many young girls were fond of. Her concern that the Princesses might have a difficult time coping with the outdoors was put to rest when Elizabeth and Margaret told her they loved getting dirty and wanted to cook sausages on sticks. At the company's first gathering, Elizabeth and Margaret came appropriately dressed for fun, while "fourteen little cousins or friends" came dressed "in their best, hairs beautifully curled and white gloves completing the bright array." The future Queen is seen above in her Girl Guides uniform.

—*British Information Services*

> **It Probably Has a Great Ending** Antony Armstrong-Jones, former husband of Princess Margaret, was once asked which book he would take with him to a desert island if he could only take one. His answer: *A History of Architecture on the Comparative Method.*

Q *Who counts Harriet Beecher Stowe, Louisa May Alcott, Ralph Waldo Emerson, Erle Stanley Gardner, and Barbara Cartland among her ancestors, and who are her favorite writers?*

A Princess Diana enjoys the works of writers Mary Stewart and Daphne du Maurier.

Q *Which two foreigners were Queen Mary's favorite authors?*
A The Russians Dostoevsky and Tolstoy.

Q *Which Russian is among Prince Charles's favorite authors?*
A He is partial to Solzhenitsyn.

Q *Which royal compiled a collection of more than 55,000 books?*
A Augustus Frederick, Duke of Sussex, and son of George III; he died in 1843.

Q *Name the two Princes of Wales accomplished at playing the banjo.*
A The present Prince of Wales, Charles, and the last Prince of Wales, Edward (future Edward VIII).

Q *Name the Queen who granted a patent for the first typewriter.*
A Queen Anne (1702–14), on January 7, 1714, to Henry Mill. The patent states, in part, that Mill "represented unto us, that he has, by his great study, paines and expense, lately invented and brought to perfection an artificial machine or method for the impressing or transcribing of letters singly or progressively one after another, as in writing, whereby all writings whatsoever may be engrossed on paper or parchment so neat and exact as not to be distinguished from print."

Q *Who was the first King to have buttons on his garments?*
A Edward II (1307–27). He ordered six pair of boots that buttoned closed from merchant Robert le Fermor of Flete Street (sic) on May 24, 1321.

Q *Identify the royal who founded the Ascot horse racing track.*
A Queen Anne (1702–14), in 1711.

Q *Who was the first Norman King of England?*

A William I, the Conqueror (1066–87), who didn't speak English. He had been Duke of Normandy.

Q *Until Edward VIII came to the throne, who was the last bachelor King?*

A William II, the Red (1087–1100), who never married.

Q Name the royal believed to be the first man to have a zipper incorporated into his pants.

A Admiral The Earl Louis Mountbatten of Burma, the uncle of Prince Philip. He is seen here toward the conclusion of World War II with General Douglas MacArthur.

—*British Information Services*

The Youngest Sovereign to rule England was Henry VI (1422–61 and 1470–71), who was nine months old when he succeeded his father, Henry V (1413–22). His mother was Katherine of Valois, France. A year after his birth Henry VI was also King of France (see related item this page).

Q *Which royal collects old lavatory seats?*

A The unusual hobbyist, and perhaps the only such collector in the world, is Prince Charles, who has more than 130 of them.

Q *Which monarch was the first to enjoy the convenience of a toilet?*

A Elizabeth I, the Virgin Queen (1558–1603), who had one installed at the encouragement of her godson, Sir John Harington, at her palace at Richmond in 1597.

Q *Identify the only person known to have ignored responding to a personal letter from the Duchess of Windsor.*

A Her third mother-in-law, Queen Mary, Consort of George V. The Duchess wrote to her at the end of World War II hoping to mend fences. The Queen did not reply.

Q *What does a person have to do to receive a yearly birthday telegram from Elizabeth II for the rest of his or her life?*

A Attain the ripe old age of 105.

Q *Which royal was denied entry to a Catholic church because it was determined she was improperly dressed?*

A Princess Margaret, in 1964. She wore a sleeveless dress that church authorities in Padua thought inappropriate for entrance.

Q *Name the Prince who was denied membership to a university club in the college he attended.*

A Prince Charles. The organization was the University Labour Club at Cambridge. Membership was denied by Lord Butler, College Master.

Q *Name the royal who resigned membership in the Explorers Club because he was shocked at the menu prepared for the annual dinner.*

A Prince Philip, who was "appalled by the exhibition of bad taste" in serving lionburgers and hippopotamus steaks, among other questionable delicacies.

Q Name the two monarchs under whom Winston Churchill served as Prime Minister.

A George VI, during the World War II years, and then in the 1950s his daughter, Elizabeth II. Churchill is seen in this wartime photo with Vice Admiral Lord Louis Mountbatten during a break in the Casablanca Conference.

—U.S. Army Air Force photo

Q Who was the first reigning monarch to visit Number 10 Downing Street?

A Elizabeth II and Prince Philip came to the Prime Minister's office-residence to attend the resignation dinner of Sir Winston Churchill in April 1955. Also seen here is Lady Churchill.

—British Information Services

Q What is extraordinary about this photo?

A The photo records a rare waiving of Court procedure inasmuch as Princess Margaret is seen walking ahead of her sister, Queen Elizabeth II. It occurred in March 1955, when Princess Margaret returned home after a triumphant Caribbean tour which covered 15,000 miles by plane and royal yacht. The Queen was so delighted with the success of Margaret's travels that she encouraged her sister to walk ahead of her at the airport and then drive ahead into London.

—*British Information Services*

> **Reformed Smoker** Prince Philip gave up smoking at the request of his new bride and reportedly had his last cigarette the night before their wedding. For some time afterwards he would satisfy the oral urge to smoke by substituting candy and, for a short time, a clothing button.

Q *Name the Queen who failed to recognize the value of an automatic knitting machine and declined to support its development.*

A Elizabeth I (1558–1603), who sent away its inventor, the Reverend William Lee. Lee died unknown and obscure years later in 1610. However, his brother took the machine and captured the support of the knitting industry, making a fortune.

Q *Name the Collie for whom Queen Victoria had a monument built at Balmoral Castle.*

A Noble, who died in 1887. He was her favorite Collie for more than fifteen years.

Q *Why did Henry VII (1485–1509) decree that all mastiff dogs be destroyed during his reign?*

A Because he had been told that the large dogs were able to kill the king of beasts, lions, and considered this a threat to royalty. Anyone caught harboring the dogs after the decree suffered severe punishment.

Q *When was the investiture of Prince Charles as Prince of Wales?*

A In 1969, at Caenarvon Castle.

Q *Which future King participated in the World War I Battle of Jutland?*

A George VI, who at the time was second in line for the throne. He would become King after his father, George V, died and his brother Edward VIII abdicated.

Q *Which monarch was particularly deft in petit point (needlework)?*

A George VI, who once made a dozen chair covers for his mother.

Q *Name the royal who designed a swivel tea kettle that Elizabeth II uses regularly.*

A Her husband, Prince Philip. He also designed the clear "bubble-top" which has been used by her in motorcades.

Q *Identify the Queen who stuffed cloth in her mouth to puff out sunken facial features and compensate for missing teeth.*

A Queen Elizabeth I (1558–1603).

Q *Identify the first King to use a gun.*

A Edward III (1327–77), who recorded using a few small weapons in 1325. The first known picture of a gun was a colored drawing made for Edward a year earlier by his chaplain, Walter de Milemete.

Makeup Helped   George VI, seen in this 1946 photo with his daughter, the future Elizabeth II, at White Lodge, Windsor, often used facial makeup to improve his usually pale coloring.

—British Information Services

Interrupted Childhoods Richard II (1377–99), son of the Black Prince and grandson of Edward III (1327–77), was nine years old when their deaths thrust him on the throne. When he was in his thirties he took as his second wife the seven-year-old Princess Isabella of France. She was a widow five years later.

Q *Which King is credited with introducing ice cream to England?*

A Charles II (1660–85), who first tasted it in Paris while in exile on the Continent and later encouraged its preparation at his Court.

Q *Which King is responsible for encouraging the use of bricks in building?*

A Henry VIII (1509–47). Although there had been brick buildings in England as early as the thirteenth century, it wasn't until his reign that they became widely used in prestigious buildings such as Hampton Court Palace.

Q *Identify the future Queen responsible for making carpets popular in England.*

A Princess Eleanor of Castile, Consort to Edward I (1272–1307), who brought Eastern carpets woven by Arabs in Spain with her when she married Prince Edward in 1225.

Q *Name the future King who encouraged and supported the development of gas lighting in England.*

A George IV (1820–30), who as Prince of Wales (and later Regent) was a major supporter of the eccentric promoter Frederick Albert Windsor, not until then taken seriously. Through George's efforts, the first street lighting began in 1814.

Q *Which royal owned three horses that won the Derby?*

A Edward VII, whose horses won in 1896 and 1900 while he was Prince of Wales and as King in 1909, the year before he died.

Q *What are the racing colors used by Elizabeth II's horse stables?*

A Blue and red.

Q *Which King established Eton College?*

A Henry VI (1422–61 and 1470–71), during his first reign in 1440.

Third Cousins   Queen Elizabeth II and her husband Prince Philip are third cousins through the lineage of Queen Victoria. They were photographed at Sandringham, the royal family's private residence in Norfolk, on the anniversary of her thirtieth year as a ruling monarch in 1982.

—British Information Services

Polo Rankings   Both Prince Philip and his son Prince Charles were avid polo players and by the standard ranking (from 2 to 10) they once held ratings of 5 and 4, respectively. Philip's enthusiasm for the sport is so intense that he once used a Royal Navy destroyer, a fast car, a plane, and another fast car after a state visit to return to Windsor so he could participate with his team in the finals of the Royal Windsor Cup. He managed to score two of his team's seven goals in the winning effort.

Q *Who was the first royal to experience the use of chloroform as an aid in childbirth?*

A Victoria, who came under its comforting effects for the first time with the birth of Prince Leopold, her eighth child, and had it administered again for her ninth and final birth, Princess Beatrice.

Q *Who was the last King to be killed in battle?*

A Richard III, Duke of Gloucester (1483–85). He was killed in the Battle of Bosworth.

Q *Who were the tallest and shortest Kings?*

A Tallest was Edward IV (1461–83), who was reportedly 6′4″. The shortest was Charles I (1625–49), who came in at 5′1″.

Q *How tall was Queen Victoria?*

A Exactly five feet.

Q *Name the last Court Dwarf kept by royalty and the royal who had him.*

A Coppernin, who amused Princess Augusta, mother of George III (1760–1820). She died in 1772, and with her the unusual tradition.

Q *Who was the shortest person ever knighted by a monarch?*

A Sir Jeffrey Hudson, a 3′9″ dwarf who was a favorite of Charles I (1625–49).

Q *Which monarch had the smallest dwarf in history?*

A Bloody Mary (1553–58), who made two-foot-tall John Jarvis her Page of Honour.

Q *Who are Michael and Caroline Terry?*

A He is Prince Andrew's valet; she is Fergie's personal maid.

> **Q** Which royal once professed an interest in becoming an astronaut?
> **A** The then six-year-old son of Elizabeth II, Prince Edward, who confessed the desire to Mike Collins, Neil Armstrong, and Buz Aldrin (left to right) when the Apollo 11 crew were guests at Buckingham Palace. They are seen above reunited in 1979 for the tenth anniversary of their voyage.
>
> *—NASA photo*

Q *Name the first royal to learn to fly.*

A The Duke of York (future George VI), who was instructed in 1919 in an Avro 504 while serving with the RAF. His older brother Edward, Prince of Wales, flew for the first time in 1929.

Q *Who once compared Prince Andrew's features to those of Robert Redford?*

A His brother, Prince Charles.

Q *Identify the Prince of Wales who shot a hole-in-one playing golf.*

A Prince Edward (future Edward VIII) in Brazil after having arrived there aboard the SS *Alcantara* in 1931.

Q *Which royal was part of a winning tennis doubles pair at Wimbledon?*

A The future George VI, while competing in the Royal Air Force Championship in 1926.

Q *If you were introduced to the Hon. Frances Shand-Kydd, who would you have just met?*

A Prince Charles's natural mother-in-law, Princess Diana's mother.

Q *Who was the last monarch to lead troops on the field of battle?*

A George II (1727–1760), who led his army in the War of Austrian Succession (1740–48), which began after Maria Theresa became the Hapsburg ruler.

Q *Name the King responsible for organizing the British postal service into a functioning source of revenue.*

A Charles I (1635–49), who appointed Thomas Witherings to initiate frequent day and night service in 1635. The first postage stamps, however, didn't come into being until 1840 during the reign of Queen Victoria.

Q *Where does the royal family traditionally spend Christmas and Easter?*

A At Windsor Castle.

Q *Which royal was once robbed of approximately $40,000 worth of jewelry?*

A The Duchess of Windsor. The jewelry was discovered missing from her room while she was a house guest of the Earl of Dudley in 1946.

First Jet Flight   The Queen Mother and Princess Margaret had their first flight in a jet aircraft aboard a British Overseas Airways Corporation's de Havilland Comet in June 1952. The four-hour trip, which took them over France, Switzerland, Italy, and the northern tip of Corsica, was under the command of Group Captain John Cunningham, de Havilland's chief test pilot. The jet covered 1,850 miles and reached a maximum speed of 510 mph at an altitude of 36,000 ft.

—British Information Services

Fact The beheaded Charles I (1625–49) was, for some unknown reason, buried in the same vault at Windsor Castle as Henry VIII. In 1813 an autopsy was conducted by Sir Henry Halford, the royal surgeon to King George III, to determine exactly whose remains were whose. Halford stole Charles's fourth cervical vertebra and used it for several years to pour salt when he had dinner guests. When Queen Victoria learned of this in 1843, she ordered the bone be returned to the King's coffin.

Q *Which monarch so disliked mustaches on the clergy that he asked bishops to issue orders forbidding them?*
A Edward VII, even though he himself sported both mustache and beard.

Q *Identify the monarch who retired each evening promptly at 11:10 P.M.*
A George V. He was actually getting in bed earlier, since he kept all clocks running ahead of time.

Q *Why did Edward VII go around destroying statues after the death of his mother, Queen Victoria?*
A Because the statues were of the Scot John Brown, the Queen's close friend and confidant (some think more) in most of the years of her widowhood and with whom Edward never got along.

Q *Name the modern-day monarch who refused to wear any pants that had creases pressed in the front.*
A George V. He thought them unfashionable.

Q *Identify the only King believed to have had a tattoo.*
A George V had been making the Royal Navy a successful career until the untimely death of his brother Prince Albert moved him a heartbeat from the throne. The tattoo, of a dragon, was acquired during his days as a naval cadet. It was on his right arm.

Q *Who was the last monarch to rule the American Colonies?*
A George III (1760–1820).

Q *Who was the last monarch to reign without the convenience of a telephone or electricity in the palace?*
A William IV (1830–37). He was followed by Victoria (1837–1901), who made use of these discoveries in the last third of her reign.

Fact It was photos like this, showing Prince Philip sporting a beard while on tour in 1957, that prompted the Queen and her ladies-in-waiting to don false beards when they met him upon arrival home. He is seen above leaving Victoria Hospital at Bathurst, Gambia, with his escort for the visit, Dr. S. H. O. Jones.

—British Information Services

Q When did Queen Elizabeth II make her first coast-to-coast tour of Canada?

A In 1951, when she was still a Princess. Her second coast-to-coast tour was in June 1959, during which she opened the St. Lawrence Seaway. In photo above, she and Prince Philip are being escorted by "Mounties" in scarlet tunics and riding motorcycles through the beflagged streets of St. John's, Newfoundland.

—British Information Services

> **Q** Which member of the royal family was tutored in driving by an Indianapolis 500 winner?
>
> **A** Prince Andrew, who was taught the finer points of driving by Graham Hill. Hill is seen here in his American Red Ball Special prior to winning the 1966 classic in just under 3 hours, 28 minutes, with an average speed of 144$^+$ mph. It was Hill's first of three appearances in the Indy 500. However, he lost "Rookie of the Year" honors at the Speedway to another British visitor, Jackie Stewart. Hill died November 29, 1975.
>
> *—Indianapolis Motor Speedway photo*

Q *Name the first reigning monarch to drive a car.*

A Edward VII, who had actually driven a car in 1897 as Prince of Wales. By the time he became King, he owned three Daimlers. His first car, a six-horse-power Daimler Model A, was later used for years by George V and taken for a "test" drive by George VI.

Q *Identify the distinctive mascot that appears as a radiator ornament on the Queen's car.*

A A silver sculpture of St. George slaying a dragon. The device was tooled to replace the standard Rolls-Royce ornament and moves to any car she travels in.

Q *Identify the royal whose Nash convertible automobile was stolen in 1960.*

A Princess Margaret. A fourteen-year-old boy took it for a joy ride while she was visiting friends for lunch. It was recovered after a speedy police chase.

Q *How many palaces, castles, and residences does the Queen own or have use of?*

A Ten in total: the palaces of Westminster, Buckingham, Holyroodhouse, St. James, Hampton, and Kensington; plus Windsor Castle; Balmoral; Sandringham; and the Tower of London.

Playhouse for a Prince During World War II three London firemen spent their spare time making toys for nurseries. Sometime afterwards they used their talents to build this 10-foot-high miniature Tudor cottage which they presented to Queen Elizabeth II for her young son, Prince Charles. The ground floor has a sitting room furnished in period style, a small staircase leading up to a dormer-windowed bedroom, and another which leads to a workroom fitted with a carpenter's bench, complete with miniature tools.

—*British Information Services*

A Banquet Fit for a King?   When the menu for Henry VI's (1422–61 and 1470–71) coronation as King of England was planned (he was also King of France), it displayed tastes that were a bit on the wild side. Soup was served to the blare of trumpets, but the noteworthy thing about it was its color (because it contained blood!) and the white lions swimming (or drowning) in the serving vats. This morbid feline attraction continued to the custard, which had young leopards sunk in it.

Q *What is the main or principal residence of the King or Queen?*

A Most people believe the answer is obviously Buckingham Palace, where they live, but that is incorrect. Westminster Palace is number one, at least officially.

Q *Which King appointed professional boxers and toughs to serve as aides during his coronation?*

A George IV (1820–30), who expected trouble from his estranged wife (and cousin) Caroline of Brunswick and her supporters. The couple had been separated since the birth of their only child in 1796, and Caroline had resided in Italy since 1814. When he learned she intended to be present at his 1821 coronation and claim her right as Queen Consort, George thought he better surround himself with muscle. She did make an appearance but was unsuccessful in attempts to enter Westminster Abbey or otherwise greatly disrupt the ceremony.

Q *Which King lost his crown on the day of his coronation?*

A Henry IV (1399–1413). It fell from his head when caught by a sudden wind as he rose to address those gathered at his outdoor banquet.

Q *Why are all swans in Britain marked or "branded" annually to protect them from the sovereign?*

A Because, under old English law, unmarked swans can be claimed as property of the King or Queen. The ceremonial marking is simply a quaint tradition.

Q *Name the Queen who replaced hand-held brooms with mechanical carpet sweepers at Buckingham Palace.*

A Queen Victoria. Though the first patent for such devices was issued in 1811, they didn't become popular until the 1870s, and made their royal appearance in 1877.

Q Name both the boat and class of the sailboat Queen Elizabeth II and Prince Philip enjoyed sailing in for several years on the river Beaulieu.

A The boat was the Dragon class yacht *Bluebottle*, seen above. Joining the Duke of Edinburgh and the young Prince of Wales on this outing was yacht designer Uffa Fox.

—*British Information Services*

The Cherry Brandy Incident   While a fourteen-year-old student at Gordonstoun School, Prince Charles slipped into a hotel bar to avoid the gawking of crowds who were watching him and other school friends as they prepared to have a meal in the hotel restaurant. Once in the bar, Charles felt conspicuous standing around and not drinking, so he impulsively ordered a cherry brandy, the first drink that came to mind. He had hardly taken a sip when he was again the center of attention. A newspaper reporter broke the story and it flashed around the world. "I was ready to pack my bags and leave for Siberia," he would recall in later years.

Q *Which member of the present royal family was at death's door in 1980?*

A Prince Charles, who collapsed after consuming ice-cold champagne following an exhausting polo match in the Florida sun. Attending medics reported that for a brief period they recorded no vital signs.

Q *Name the monarch who once consumed so much brandy and soda that it was necessary to use a stomach pump on him.*

A Edward VIII. Known as a heavy drinker, this particular incident took place during the Abdication crisis in December 1936.

Q *Name the royal who drowned in a vat of wine.*

A George, Duke of Clarence, who was murdered in 1478. He was an older brother of the Duke of Gloucester (future Richard III).

Q *To which Prince of Wales did doctors suggest that permitting pigeons to nip his feet would cure typhus?*

A Prince Henry, son of James I and VI and Princess Anne of Denmark. He died in 1612 at the age of eighteen.

Q *Why did Queen Alexandra, wife of Edward VII, often wear high-necked clothing?*

A Because she was extremely self-conscious of a childhood throat scar and tried to conceal it.

Q *Identify one particular type of clothing Elizabeth II always takes on trips.*

A A black dress and accessories in the event a death occurs. This permits her to be properly dressed immediately. Her packing also includes black-edged writing paper.

Q Identify the type of aircraft flown by Prince Charles in his first public demonstration as a pilot.

A A fully qualified helicopter pilot in the Royal Navy, Charles is seen here doing a pre-flight check on the Wessex Mark V. He flew before 30,000 people during International Air Day at the Royal Naval Air Station, Culdrose, England.

—British Information Services

> **Anti-Smoking Lobby**   The first sovereign to go on record as being opposed to smoking was James I and VI (1567–1625), who believed that Indians in the American Colonies had wrongfully thought the use of tobacco would cure venereal diseases.

Q *Which Prince of Wales made the following unromantic observation about marriage: "It is the last decision on which I would want my head to be ruled by my heart"?*

A Prince Charles.

Q *Which member of the current royal family is afraid of the dark?*

A Princess Margaret Rose.

Q *Which King was once confined in a straitjacket?*

A George III (1760–1820), who, like Queen Anne before him, was afflicted with porphyria which at the time was confused with mental disorder. The King and his family protested suggestions that he abdicate, and he refused to perform any duties as monarch until he was released.

Q *Which royal is credited with making dinner jackets popular?*

A Edward VII, who also set trends by wearing Homburg hats and knickers.

Q *Which royal once dressed as a beatnik for a costume party?*

A Elizabeth II, in 1962. Do you remember beatniks? Before yuppies and yippies, we had hippies; before hippies there were beatniks.

Q *Which royal made the bowler a popular hat in America?*

A Edward VIII, as Prince of Wales in the 1920s.

Q *Who was the last monarch to regularly enjoy oysters?*

A Edward VIII. The tradition of including oysters on the royal menu, which had begun in 1830 with the reign of William IV (1830–37), ended when George VI came to the throne. The ban still continues since Elizabeth II dislikes them as much as her father did.

Q *When did Elizabeth II officially curtsey for the last time?*

A In 1952, in respect to the remains of her late father, George VI, as he lay in state at St. George's Chapel, Windsor, before burial there.

Q *Name the royal who won $225 the very first time she played poker.*
A The future Duchess of Windsor, as Mrs. Wallis Warfield Simpson.

Q Which royal worked for two days in 1946 as a waiter in London's famous Savoy Hotel?

A The son of the Earl of Airlie, Angus Ogilvy, who was one of several volunteers who temporarily joined the staff during a post–World War II labor dispute. His career in that field ended abruptly when he dropped an omelette at the feet of an important guest. He and his wife, Princess Alexandra, are seen above in this 1981 photo.

—British Information Services

> **Better than "Off with Their Heads!"** After once discovering what was thought to be lice on his dinner plate, George III (1760–1820) ordered that all who worked in the royal kitchen should have bald or clean-shaven heads.

Q *Name the first royal (by birth) to take a nonroyal job.*

A Prince William of Gloucester (1941–72), who joined a London banking firm in 1965. A first cousin of Queen Elizabeth II, he was killed in a private plane crash in August 1972.

Q *Name the first monarch to go bankrupt.*

A Edward III (1327–77) was unable to repay a $7-million loan in 1339. Much of the money had been used to finance war with France (the Hundred Years' War).

Q *Which monarch installed her personal astrologer as chancellor of St. Paul's?*

A Elizabeth I (1558–1603), as a reward for his astrological readings for her. He used a crystal ball.

Q *Which royal once asked U.S. President Harry S. Truman for his autograph?*

A George VI, when the two met for lunch aboard the British battle cruiser *Renown* shortly after the Potsdam Conference.

Q *Identify the first King to imprint his signature with a wooden stamp.*

A Henry VI, Duke of Cornwall (1422–61 and 1470–71). He was deposed in 1461, returned to the throne briefly in 1470, and was killed in 1471.

Q *Who was the first member of the royal family to attend a Rugby League game?*

A Edward, Prince of Wales (future Edward VIII), on November 23, 1932, in Central Park, Wigan.

Q *Which royal-by-marriage had an ancestor canonized as a saint in the Roman Catholic Church in the 1970s?*

A Angus Ogilvy, who is married to the Queen's cousin, Princess Alexandra. The ancestor is St. John Ogilvy.

Q What is the occupation description that appears on Prince Philip's passport?

A It indicates that he is gainfully employed as Prince of the Royal Household. When this 1951 photo was taken in the Mediterranean, however, he was a lieutenant commander in the Royal Navy, commanding HMS *Magpie*. (Note: Since all British passports are technically issued by the sovereign, Elizabeth II herself does not have, nor need, one.)

—*British Information Services*

> **Sent to America as Punishment** George III's wife, Queen Charlotte, once caught a household servant dressing up in the Queen's clothes and jewels. The King found this so serious an affront that he ordered the woman exiled to the American Colonies. However, once in America she passed herself off as the Queen's sister, Princess Susanna, for nearly two years before being recognized.

Q *Which royal holds British passport #1?*

A Prince Philip.

Q *Identify the monarch who, while in poor health, actually placed a bet that he would live a year.*

A George II (1727–60), who made the bet after learning that bookmakers in London were giving 10 to 1 odds that the king would die within the year. He won.

Q *Which royal hung a sign "Lavatory Under Repair" on the door of a smoking room in an effort to conceal the room from the Queen?*

A Edward, Prince of Wales, during his mother, Queen Victoria's, first visit to his new home, Marlborough House. The Queen strongly disliked smoking. The ruse worked.

Q *Name the female member of the royal family who has driven railroad train engines on three separate continents.*

A Elizabeth II, who was Princess Elizabeth when she drove trains in England, Canada, and Africa.

Q *Identify the King whose departure after a foreign state visit was delayed because of an argument over who would drive the train.*

A Edward VIII, during the land portion of the now infamous September 1936 tour that included the cruise on the *Nahlin*. Edward's host in Bulgaria was King Boris, who prided himself as a railroad buff and insisted on driving the train. The King's contender for the honor was his brother, also a train buff!

Q *Identify the European head of state who provided a special train for the Prince of Wales in 1928 so Edward could quickly make his way across Europe and return home after learning that his father, George V, was seriously ill?*

A Italian dictator Benito Mussolini. George V, however, did not die until eight years later.

Q How are the ampulla and anointing spoon, both part of the Crown
Jewels, used in the coronation ceremony of a monarch?

A The ampulla, which takes the form of an eagle with outstretched
wings, is actually a receptacle for holy oil. The oil flows through
the beak onto the anointing spoon and is then administered to the
King or Queen being crowned.

—British Information Services

Q *Which royal made this sarcastic remark to an aide the first time he saw the woman he was to marry: "I'm not well. Get me a glass of Brandy!"?*

A George IV (1820–30), upon meeting his future second wife, Princess Caroline, daughter of the Duke of Brunswick. The marriage had been arranged in order to "right" the wrong done by his first marriage to the twice-previously-married Maria Fitzherbert. That union was contrary to the Royal Marriages Act of 1772.

Q *Between which two Queens did the following conversation take place: "As we're Queens together we can say what we please"?*

A Queen Victoria, upon meeting the ten-year-old Queen of the Netherlands, Wilhelmina, who visited her at Windsor Castle in 1895. After lunch, however, the indulgent Victoria turned to her young royal guest and asked: "And what can we do to amuse you now, my child?"

Q *Name the King who later admitted that by the time he was seventeen years old he had become "rather too fond of women and wine."*

A George IV (1820–30).

Q *Name the sovereign who founded Trinity College at Oxford.*

A Henry VIII (1509–47), the year before he died. The University of Dublin, also known as Trinity College, was founded in 1591 by Queen Elizabeth I.

Q *Which King was believed to have been an albino?*

A Edward the Confessor (1042–66), who was canonized a saint by the Roman Catholic Church in 1161. He was the last true Anglo-Saxon to reign.

Q *Which royal said the following about a museum sculpture in San Francisco: "It looks like something to hang a towel on"?*

A Prince Philip, who also once commented that a Henry Moore sculpture reminded him of a "monkey's gallstone."

Q *Which royal had this opinion of the ruins in Rome: "Look at two mouldering stones and someone tells you they are the temple of something!"*

A Edward, Prince of Wales (future Edward VII).

Q *Identify the King and Queen who have reigned the shortest amount of time.*

A Queen Jane (1553), the former Lady Jane Grey, who at age fifteen was nominally Queen for nine days in 1553. She was imprisoned after her second cousin Mary succeeded her. Even though Jane had said the crown belonged to Mary all along, Bloody Mary had her beheaded the following year. The shortest reign by a King belongs to Edward V (1483), who tallied up seventy-seven days before his uncle the Duke of Gloucester managed to have Edward (and Edward's brother Richard) declared illegitimate and thereby gain the throne for himself as Richard III. The third shortest reign belongs to Elizabeth II's uncle, Edward VIII, who abdicated.

Q *Name the King and Queen who have reigned the longest.*

A The longest reign by either a King or Queen was Queen Victoria's (1837–1901), which lasted sixty-three years. The longest reigning King was George III (1760–1820), at fifty-nine years. (At this writing Elizabeth II enjoys the tenth longest reign.)

First Glider Flight   Prince Philip is seen here in the cockpit of a Slingsby T-42 prior to his first glider flight in May 1957. Also aboard, but not visible in photo, was instructor Peter Collier.

—British Information Services

Q *Which royal said visiting Morocco was "like being kidnapped"?*

A Princess Margaret, who apparently found her visit quite adventurous.

Q *What does Prince Philip think about the red carpet tradition?*

A He considers use of the carpet "silly" and has said: "The person who thought up the red carpet should have their head examined." Another version of the above substitutes "man" for "person" and "invented" for "thought up."

Q *Which royal once told a group of Scottish women that "British women can't cook"?*

A Prince Philip, in 1966.

Q *What beach was Prince Charles talking about when he compared it to "swimming in sewage"?*

A St. Kilda, Australia. He made the unflattering remark after experiencing it in 1970.

Q *Which royal believed that politicians who advocated worldwide disarmament were ill-advised and guilty of preaching "rubbish and nonsense"?*

A Edward, Prince of Wales (future Edward VII).

Q *Who said: "The average family wouldn't know what hit them if their daughter married the future King"?*

A Earl Spencer, father of Princess Diana.

Q *Which royal likened the marriage of a daughter to "taking a poor lamb to be sacrificed"?*

A Queen Victoria. The remark was made prior to the marriage of her daughter, Princess Royal Victoria Adelaide, to the future King of Prussia and Emperor of Germany, Frederick III.

Q *Which royal hoped out loud that a news photographer who had fallen from a tree "breaks his bloody neck"?*

A Prince Philip, during a trip to India in 1961 when he thought the press was being particularly annoying.

Q *Which royal said about a future King: "His intellect is of no more use than a pistol packed in the bottom of a trunk"?*

A Prince Albert, about his son, the future Edward VII.

A BENNY HILL PRODUCTION?

Despite the image of tradition and efficiency captured forever on film when Elizabeth II was crowned, not all previous coronations went so smoothly.

For instance, when George III (1760–1820) and Queen Consort Charlotte Sophia were crowned in September 1761, more things nearly went wrong than went right:

• The original coronation date, September 20, came and went as all work stopped while craftsmen and laborers argued over jurisdiction, authority, and other matters.

• Visiting foreign dignitaries and the Archbishop of Canterbury, Thomas Secker, were pressed into service to hunt for the Chair of State (which had been "borrowed" by a cleric who had no chair in his room).

• It was discovered that the jeweled State Sword, with its scabbard studded with sapphires, rubies, and diamonds, was also missing. For this search the King himself got involved and it was recovered, simply having been misplaced.

• Hardly an hour before the ceremony was to begin, Queen Charlotte Sophia asked the Lord High Steward why the canopy had not been installed. It was discovered everybody thought someone else was doing it.

• During the just over six-hour service at Westminster Abbey, food was served . . . and glasses and trays of plates dropped while the Archbishop spoke.

• Afterwards the King's Champion, who was supposed to ride into the banquet dramatically and cast a gauntlet before the monarch, had difficulties with the rented show horse, who sashayed past the King in reverse!

• Actors who had been hired to impersonate foreign royals who did not attend became drunk and blurted out who they really were.

Otherwise the coronation went off without a hitch.

Appendixes

BIRTHDAYS AND ASTROLOGICAL SIGNS OF QUEEN ELIZABETH II's FAMILY

NAME	DATE	SIGN
George VI (deceased)	December 14, 1895	Sagittarius
Elizabeth, the Queen Mother	August 4, 1900	Leo
Elizabeth II	April 21, 1926	Taurus
Prince Philip, Duke of Edinburgh	June 10, 1921	Gemini
Prince Charles, Prince of Wales	November 14, 1948	Scorpio
Diana, Princess of Wales	July 1, 1961	Cancer
Prince William	June 21, 1982	Cancer
Prince Henry	September 15, 1984	Virgo
Princess Anne	August 15, 1950	Leo
Mark Phillips	September 22, 1948	Virgo
Peter Phillips	November 15, 1977	Scorpio
Zara Phillips	May 15, 1981	Taurus
Prince Andrew, Duke of York	February 19, 1960	Aquarius
Sarah, Duchess of York	October 15, 1959	Libra
Prince Edward	March 10, 1964	Pisces
Princess Margaret, Countess of Snowdon	August 21, 1930	Leo
David, Viscount Linley	November 3, 1961	Scorpio
Lady Sarah	May 1, 1964	Taurus

THE KINGS AND QUEENS SINCE 829

Britain has had 108 monarchs between Alpin (c. 837) in the north and Ecgbert (829–39) in the south, and including the reigning sovereign, Elizabeth II. Before Scotland and England were unified under one monarch, Scots ruled in the north for 766 years, while Anglo-Saxons (and briefly Danes) ruled for 237 years in the south. The Normans ended Anglo domination of the south in 1066 and themselves ruled for another 537 years (there were also three coinciding reigns by Welsh Kings not shown in the chart: Gruffydd, 1039–63; Llywelyn the Great, 1194–1240; and Llywelyn the Last, 1246–82). Finally, in the person of James I and VI (of England and Scotland) the north and south were unified in 1603 under one sovereign. That royal line still exists today. The vertical listings can be cross-read to better appreciate coinciding reigns.

THE SCOTS	THE ANGLO-SAXONS AND DANES
Alpin, died circa 837	Ecgbert, 829–39
Kenneth, 839–60, killed	Aethelwulf, 839–856, abdicated
Donald I, 860–62	Aethelbald, 856–60
Constantine I, 862–77, killed in battle	Aethelbert, 860–66
Aedh, 877–78, killed in battle	Aethelred I, 866–71
Queen Eocha, 878–89, deposed	Alfred, the Great, 871–99
Donald II, 889–900, killed in battle	Eadward, the Elder, 900–24
Constantine II, 900–42, abdicated	Aethelstan, 924–39
Malcolm I, 943–954, killed in battle	Eadmund I, 939–46, murdered
Indulf, 954–62, abdicated	Eadred, 946–55
Dubh, 962–66, killed in battle	Edwy, the Fair, 955–59
Cuilean, 966–71, killed	Eadgar, the Peaceful, 959–75
Kenneth II, 971–95, murdered	Eadward, the Martyr, 875–78,
Constantine III, 995–97, killed	murdered
Kenneth III, 997–1005, killed in battle	Aethelred II, the Unready, 978–1013,
Malcolm II, 1005–34	deposed
Duncan I, 1034–40, killed	(D) Svegn, King of Denmark &
Macbeth, 1040–57, killed in battle	Norway, 1013–14
Lulach, 1057–58, killed in battle	Aethelred II (resumed), 1014–16
Malcolm III, 1058–93	Eadmund II, 1016
Donald Bane, 1093–May 1094,	(D) Cnut, King of Denmark & Norway,
deposed	1016–35
Duncan II, May–November 1094,	(D) Harold I, 1037–40
killed	(D) Hardecnut, King of Denmark,
Donald Bane, 1094–97, deposed again	1040–42
Edgar, 1097–1107	Edward, the Confessor, 1042–66
Alexander I, 1107–24	(D) Harold II, 1066, killed in battle

THE SCOTS

David I, 1124–53
Malcolm IV, 1153–65, killed
William I, the Lion, 1165–1214, killed
Alexander II, 1214–49
Alexander III, 1249–86, killed
Queen Margaret, Maid of Norway,
    1286–90
* void 1291: 13 contenders for throne
John Balliol, 1292–96, forced to
    abdicate
* void 1297–1305: English rule
Robert I, the Bruce, 1306–29
David II, 1329–32, exiled in 1334
Edward Balliol, 1332–36
David II, resumed 1336–71
    (Regent: Robert the Steward 1338–
    41 & 46–57)
Robert II, 1371–90 (former Regent)
Robert III, 1390–1406
James I, 1406–37, murdered
    (Regent: Robert Stewart, 1406–20)
    (Regent: Murdac Stewart, 1420–24)
James II, 1437–60, killed
James III, 1460–88, killed
James IV, 1488–1513, killed in battle
James V, 1513–42
Queen Mary, 1542–67, abdicated
James VI, 1567–1625 (of Scotland) . . .
    who was also . . .

THE NORMANS

William I, the Conqueror, 1066–87
William II, the Red, 1097–1100, killed
Henry I, Lion of Justice, 1100–35
Stephen, 1135–54
Henry II, 1154–89
Richard I, the Lionheart, 1189–99,
    killed
John, the Lackland, 1199–1216
Henry III, 1216–72
Edward I, Longshanks, 1272–1307
Edward II, 1307–27, murdered
Edward III, 1327–77
Richard II, 1377–99, deposed
Henry IV, 1399–1413
Henry V, 1413–22
Henry VI, 1422–61, deposed
Edward IV, 1461–70, deposed
Henry VI (resumed), 1470–71, killed
Edward IV (resumed), 1471–83
Edward V, 1483 (April–June)
Richard III, 1483–85, killed in battle
Henry VII, 1485–1509
Henry VIII, 1509–47
Edward VI, 1547–53
Queen Jane, 1553 (9 days)
Queen Mary I, Bloody, 1553–58
Queen Elizabeth I, 1558–1603
James I, 1603–26 (of England)

Charles I, 1626–49, executed
* Oliver Cromwell, ruled as Lord Protector, 1653–58
Charles II, 1649–85
James II, 1685–88, deposed
Queen Mary II, 1689–94, and William III, 1689–1702
Queen Anne, 1702–14
George I, 1714–27
George II, 1727–60
George III, 1760–1820
George IV, 1820–30
William IV, 1830–37
Queen Victoria, 1837–1901
Edward VII, 1901–10
George V, 1910–36
Edward VIII, 1936, abdicated
George VI, 1936–52
Elizabeth II, 1952–

THE ROYAL FAMILY AND DESCENDANTS OF QUEEN VICTORIA

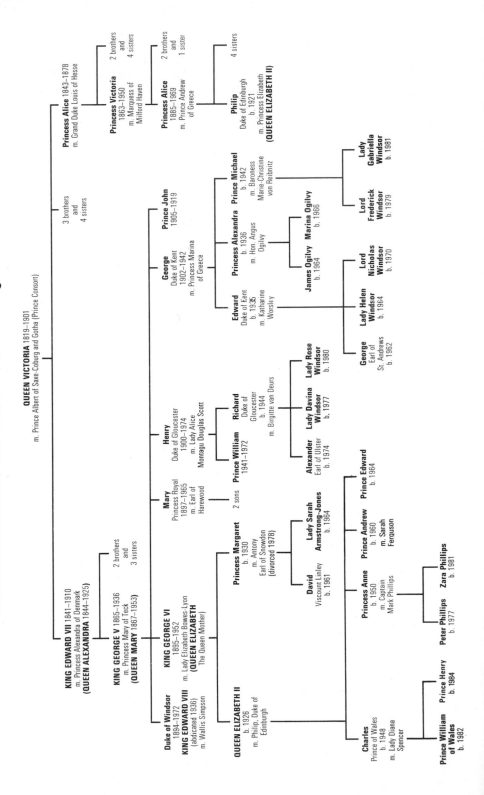

ORDER OF SUCCESSION TO THE THRONE

(as of January 1987)

In the Order of Succession the sons of the Sovereign and their descendants have precedence over the daughters. The daughters and their descendants have precedence over lateral lines.

1. HRH The Prince of Wales
2. HRH The Prince William of Wales
3. HRH Prince Henry
4. HRH The Prince Andrew
5. HRH The Prince Edward
6. HRH The Princess Anne
7. Peter Phillips
8. Zara Phillips
9. HRH The Princess Margaret
10. Viscount Linley
11. Lady Sarah Armstrong-Jones
12. HRH The Duke of Gloucester
13. Earl of Ulster
14. Lady Davina Windsor
15. Lady Rose Windsor
16. The Duke of Kent
17. Earl of St. Andrews
18. Lord Nicholas Windsor
19. Lady Helen Windsor
20. Lord Frederick Windsor
21. Lady Gabriella Windsor
22. Princess Alexandra
23. James Ogilvy
24. Marina Ogilvy
25. The Earl of Harewood
26. Viscount Lascelles
27. Alexander Lascelles
28. Hon. James Lascelles
29. Rowan Lascelles
30. Sophie Lascelles
31. Hon. Robert Lascelles
32. Hon. Gerald Lascelles
33. Henry Lascelles
34. The Duke of Fife
35. The Earl of Macduff
36. Lady Alexandra Carnegie
37. HM King Olav V of Norway
38. HRH Crown Prince Harald of Norway
39. HRH Prince Haakon Magnus of Norway
40. HRH Princess Martha Louise of Norway
41. Princess Ragnhild, Mrs. Lorentzen
42. Haakon Lorentzen
43. Ingeborg Lorentzen
44. Ragnhild Lorentzen
45. Princess Astrid, Mrs. Ferner
46. Alexander Ferner
47. Carl Christian Ferner
48. Cathrine Ferner
49. Benedicte Ferner
50. Elisabeth Ferner
51. HRH Princess Margarita of Rumania
52. HRH Princess Helen of Rumania
53. HRH Princess Irina of Rumania
54. HRH Princess Sophie of Rumania
55. HRH Princess Maria of Rumania
56. HRH Prince Tomislav of Yugoslavia
57. HRH Prince Nikola of Yugoslavia

FUNCTIONS OF THE MONARCH TODAY*

The terms "the Sovereign" (or "Monarch") and "the Crown," although related, are quite distinct. The Sovereign is the person on whom the Crown is constitutionally conferred, while the Crown (which represents both the Sovereign and the Government) is the symbol of supreme executive power. The Crown is vested in the Queen but in general its functions are exercised by ministers responsible to Parliament. The Queen reigns, but does not rule. The United Kingdom is governed by Her Majesty's Government in the name of the Queen. There are, however, many important acts of government which still require the participation of the Queen.

The Queen summons, prorogues (discontinues until the next session without dissolving) and dissolves Parliament. Normally she opens the new session with a speech from the throne outlining her Government's programme. When she is unable to be present, the Queen's speech is read by the Lord Chancellor. Before a Bill which has passed all its stages in both Houses of Parliament becomes a legal enactment, it must receive the Royal Assent, which is announced to both Houses. The Queen presides over meetings of the Privy Council at which, among other things, Orders in Council made under the royal prerogative (see below) or under statute are approved.

As the "fountain of justice," the Queen can, on ministerial advice, pardon or show mercy to those convicted of crimes. All criminal prosecutions on indictment are brought in the name of the Crown. In law the Queen as a private person can do no wrong, nor, being immune from civil or criminal proceedings, can she be sued in courts of law. This personal immunity, which does not extend to other members of the royal family, was expressly retained in the Crown Proceedings Act 1947, which for the first time allowed the Crown (in effect, a government department or minister) to be sued directly in civil proceedings.

As the "fountain of honour," the Queen confers peerages, knighthoods and other honours (on the recommendation of the Prime Minister who usually seeks the view of others). She makes appointments to many important state offices, on the advice of the Prime Minister or, in some cases, the appropriate Cabinet Minister. She appoints and dismisses, for instance, government ministers, judges (the dismissal of judges is regulated by statute), members of the diplomatic corps and colonial officials. As Commander-in-Chief of the armed services she appoints

---

* The text on pages 226–234 is reprinted from *The Monarchy in Britain*, prepared and published by British Information Services.

officers, and as Supreme Governor of the established Church of England she makes appointments to its bishoprics and some other senior offices.

In international affairs, the Queen (to whom foreign diplomatic representatives in London present their credentials) has the power to conclude treaties, to declare war and to make peace, to recognise foreign states and governments, and to annexe and cede territory.

THE CIVIL LIST

The basic Civil List is paid automatically by the Treasury from the Consolidated Fund under an Act of Parliament, normally passed within six months of the beginning of a reign, which continues in force for six months after the death of the Sovereign (although a revision may take place in the course of a reign). In exchange, the Sovereign surrenders to the Exchequer the revenue from the Crown Estate* and certain hereditary revenues.

The Civil List covers expenditure on the salaries and expenses of the Royal Household (staff of the Household are almost entirely paid and pensioned† on a basis analogous to that in the Civil Service), and royal bounty, alms and special services. About three-quarters of the Civil List provision is required for the salaries of those who deal with . . . State papers and correspondence, organising State occasions, visits and other public engagements in Britain and overseas, and arranging the interviews and investitures undertaken by the Queen, and those who clean and staff the royal buildings and who work in the Royal Mews.

Because of the rising costs of running the Royal Household in times of inflation, and despite every effort to make economies, it became impractical to settle the amount of the Civil List by legislation at relatively infrequent intervals. Accordingly, the Civil List Act 1975 established a system whereby payments additional to those provided under the Civil List Act 1972 could be made, subject to annual authorisation by Parliament, together with other departmental expenditure.

---

* The Crown Estate, comprising properties throughout Great Britain, traditionally belongs to the Sovereign "in right of the Crown," and is quite separate from his or her personal property. Under the Crown Estate Act 1961 management of the estate is the responsibility of commissioners appointed by the Sovereign on the advice of the Prime Minister. An annual report on the estate is submitted to Parliament.

† Payment of pensions to retired staff of the Royal Household is made by the Treasury direct from the Consolidated Fund. Parliament has also authorised payment of "Civil List pensions" which are nowadays awarded at the discretion of the Prime Minister for services to science, literature, music or the arts.

Q How much is Prince Andrew's annual stipend?
A Upon his marriage to Sarah Ferguson, the Prince's royal stipend
rose to £35,000 (about $52,000).

—*British Information Services*

Under this Act, the Treasury makes annual payments from money provided by Parliament to supplement the Queen's Civil List, annuities to certain named members of the royal family (see below), contributions towards the expenses of other members of the royal family, and Civil List pensions. The payments are by way of grant-in-aid to the Royal Trustees (the Prime Minister, the Chancellor of the Exchequer and the Keeper of the Privy Purse) and are subject to the normal parliamentary 'supply' procedure for the approval of government expenditure. The Royal Trustees generally review the working of the Civil List system at least once every ten years, and report to Parliament.

This change in the machinery for determining Civil List payments was accompanied by an offer from the Queen, which the Government accepted, to pay from 1976 onwards an annual contribution equivalent to the provision made from public funds towards the official expenses of members of the royal family for whom Parliament had made no specific provision (at present the Duke of Gloucester, the Duke of Kent and Princess Alexandra).

The amounts payable from central funds under the Civil List Acts to members of the royal family are as follows in the calendar year 1986:

The Queen's Civil List	£4,136,800
Queen Elizabeth the Queen Mother	£359,100
The Duke of Edinburgh	£200,300
Princess Anne	£124,800
Prince Andrew	£20,000
Prince Edward	£20,000
Princess Margaret	£121,500
Princess Alice, Duchess of Gloucester	£49,200
The Duke of Gloucester	£97,800
The Duke of Kent	£132,000
Princess Alexandra	£125,800

The 1972 Act provided that the younger sons of the Queen (Prince Andrew and Prince Edward) should receive £20,000 annually on reaching the age of 18, and before marriage. This would be increased to £52,000 after marriage. Prince Edward, the youngest, is to receive £14,000 of his allocation for 1986, the balance being accumulated by the Royal Trustees.

In addition the Act provides that a widow of the Prince of Wales would be entitled to an allowance of £60,000 a year and that the annual amount payable to a future wife of a younger son of the Queen in the event of her surviving her husband would be £20,000.

Any of these payments may be supplemented by the Royal Trustees under the provisions of the 1975 Act. The greater part is paid to meet official expenses incurred in carrying out public duties.

Parliament makes no special provision for the Prince of Wales, who is entitled, as Duke of Cornwall, to the net revenues of the estate of the Duchy of Cornwall—about 52,205 hectares (129,000 acres) in south-west England and London. At the age of 21 he became entitled to these revenues but voluntarily undertook to surrender half to the Exchequer. . . . On his marriage in July 1981, by agreement with the Government of the day, the voluntary surrender was reduced to a quarter.

SUCCESSION

The title to the Crown derives partly from statute, partly from common law rules of descent. The English Act of Settlement 1700 laid down that lineal Protestant descendants of Princess Sophia are alone eligible to succeed. This was affirmed by the Union of Scotland Act 1707. Subsequent Succession to the Crown Acts have confirmed this declaration; and, although the succession is not bound to continue in its present line, it can only be altered (under a provision of the Statute of Westminster 1931) by common consent of all the member nations of the Commonwealth of which the Queen is Sovereign.

The sons of the Sovereign and their descendants have precedence over daughters in succeeding to the throne. However, the daughters take precedence over descendants of the Sovereign's brothers. When a daughter succeeds, she becomes Queen Regnant and the Crown's powers are vested in her as though she were king. While the consort of a king takes her husband's rank and style, the constitution has never given any special rank or privileges to the husband of a Queen Regnant, and any honour granted to him comes from the Crown as "the fountain of honour." In practice he fills an important role in the life of the nation, as does the Duke of Edinburgh.

ACCESSION

The Sovereign succeeds to the throne as soon as his or her predecessor dies and there is no interregnum. (This automatic succession is summed up in the phrase, "the King is dead; long live the King!") He or she is at once proclaimed at an Accession Council to which all members of the Privy Council are summoned. Members of the House of Lords (including those bishops of the Church of England who sit in the House of Lords), the Lord Mayor and aldermen and other leading citizens of the City of London, and the High Commissioners in London of member nations of the Commonwealth are also invited to attend. The duration of Parliament is not affected by the death of a monarch.

CORONATION

The Sovereign's coronation follows the accession, after an interval. It does not affect the legal powers of the Crown (King Edward VIII, for instance, was never crowned but reigned for nearly a year). It is a ceremony which has remained essentially the same over a thousand years, even if details have often been modified to conform to the customs of the time. It consists broadly of recognition and acceptance of the new monarch by the people; taking by the monarch of an oath of royal duties; celebration of Holy Communion followed by anointing and crowning; and rendering of homage by the Lords Spiritual and Temporal. The service used at the coronation of Queen Elizabeth II in 1953 was derived from that used at the coronation of King Edgar at Bath in 973.

THE QUEEN'S STYLE AND TITLES

The development of the royal style and titles can be traced through a variety of changes reflecting historical events in the kingdoms of England and Scotland, in the union of those kingdoms in 1707, in the union with Ireland in 1801, and in the development of the Commonwealth. Today they are such as may be determined by the Crown under the authority of the Royal Titles Act 1953 and previous legislation. The Queen's title in the United Kingdom is: "Elizabeth the Second, by the Grace of God of the United Kingdom of Great Britain and Northern Ireland and of Her other Realms and Territories Queen, Head of the Commonwealth, Defender of the Faith." The form of the royal title is varied for the other member nations of the Commonwealth in which the Queen is head of State to suit the particular circumstances of each; all these forms include, however, the phrase "Head of the Commonwealth."

THE ROYAL FAMILY'S STYLES AND TITLES

The first son (the Heir Apparent) born to a reigning monarch is by birth Duke of Cornwall in the peerage of England, and Duke of Rothesay, Earl of Carrick and Baron of Renfrew in the peerage of Scotland; he is also Lord of the Isles and Prince and Great Steward, or Seneschal, of

Scotland. The titles "Prince of Wales" and "Earl of Chester" are created in each case, but have usually though not invariably been conferred on the Sovereign's eldest son; they were conferred on Prince Charles, the present heir, in 1958.

There is no style for an Heir or Heiress Presumptive (that is, the Prince or Princess who would succeed to the throne if the Sovereign had no son). It is usual for a Prince in that position to possess a royal dukedom. However, an Heiress Presumptive has no claim to the Duchy of Cornwall, nor can she become Princess of Wales.

The title of "Royal Highness" is accorded by Letters Patent to all the monarch's children, the children of the monarch's sons, and the eldest living son of the eldest son of the Prince of Wales. The title is enjoyed by the wives of the Royal Highnesses.

Under the Royal Marriages Act 1772 there are restrictions upon the right of descendants of King George II to marry without the monarch's consent. Until the age of 25 the consent is necessary (except in the case of the children of princesses who have married into foreign families), but after that age a marriage can take place without the consent after a year's notice to the Privy Council, unless Parliament expressly disapproves.

THE ROYAL YACHT *BRITANNIA*

The royal yacht *Britannia,* named and launched by the Queen at Clydebank (Scotland) in 1953, serves as an official and private residence for the Queen and other members of the royal family when they are engaged on visits overseas or are voyaging in home waters. The yacht also takes part in some naval exercises and undertakes routine hydrographic tasks while at sea. Designed to replace the 50-year-old *Victoria and Albert, Britannia* could be converted to hospital ship in wartime.

Her gross tonnage is 5,769 tons (5,862 tonnes) and her continuous seagoing speed is 21 knots (10·8 metres per second). Refits and docking usually take place in the Royal Dockyard at Portsmouth.

The royal apartments are aft on the shelter deck and the royal staff accommodation is on the lower deck. The royal state apartments contain some of the furniture from the *Victoria and Albert.* The Queen and the Duke of Edinburgh took a personal interest in the interior decorations, the choice of furnishings and the general fitting-out of the royal yacht.

The yacht is an independent command, administered personally by the Flag Officer Royal Yachts. He is normally appointed as an extra equerry to the Queen and, as such, is a member of the Royal Household.

Britannia's crew numbers 22 officers and 254 men when members of the royal family are embarked or when the vessel undertakes a long ocean voyage. Officers are normally appointed for two-year periods of duty. Two-thirds of the ratings are permanent crew members and remain attached to the ship for the rest of their service careers; the others are attached to the yacht for two-year periods only. They are all volunteers from the Royal Navy, but receive no special benefits in terms of pay, allowances or leave. Traditions of dress aboard the royal yacht include the wearing by seamen of naval uniform with the jumper inside the top of the trousers, which are finished at the back with a black silk bow. On all blue uniforms ratings wear white badges instead of the red which are customary in the Royal Navy. So far as is possible orders on the upper deck are executed without spoken words or commands, and by long tradition the customary naval mark of respect of piping the side is normally paid only to the Queen.

THE QUEEN'S FLIGHT

The Queen's Flight was created in 1936 (as the King's Flight) by King Edward VIII to provide air transport for the royal family's official duties. Based at Benson in Oxfordshire, the Flight is equipped with three twin-turboprop Hawker Siddeley Andover CC Mk 2 passenger transport aircraft and two Westland Wessex HCC 4 helicopters.

Provided by the Royal Air Force, the Flight operates under a general policy agreed between the Treasury and the Ministry of Defence. The Queen, the Queen Mother, the Duke of Edinburgh and the Prince of Wales are entitled to use it on all occasions. At the Queen's discretion it is also made available to other members of the royal family, but only on official duties. The Flight is used for official purposes by the Prime Minister and certain other people, such as senior ministers or visiting heads of State. The Ministry of Defence is responsible for all flights and routes of the aircraft of the Queen's Flight. The main cost of the Flight is borne on defence votes.

THE REGALIA

The regalia, or crown jewels, are the emblems of royalty and have held the same significance for the Kings and Queens of England for a thousand years. They symbolise the sense of continuity which the monarchy provides for the nation, and still have an important and valued place in the British heritage.

Since the coronation of King Charles II the regalia have been kept in the Tower of London under the guardianship of the Keeper of the Jewel House except when they are required for the coronation ceremony, in which they have a deep ritual significance. Most of the crown jewels on display at the Tower were made after the restoration of King Charles II in 1660, the previous regalia having been broken up and sold during the Republic of 1649–60. Two items which survived are the gilded silver Anointing Spoon and the gold Ampulla in the shape of an eagle, which holds the oil. In addition to the Imperial State Crown, with its thousands of precious stones, and to St. Edward's Crown, with which the Sovereign is crowned, the other principal items of the regalia include the Jewelled State Sword and the Golden Spurs symbolising knightly chivalry, the Coronation Ring, the Golden Bracelets, the Golden Orb, surmounted by a jewelled cross signifying the Sovereign's obedience to the Christian faith, and the two sceptres; the Royal Sceptre with the Cross, which contains at the end of the golden bar the Star of Africa, the largest cut diamond in the world, and the Sceptre with the Dove— the first is a symbol of kingly power and justice, the second is one of equity and mercy.

FOUR CORONATIONS EACH

Two Archbishops of Canterbury have each presided over four separate coronations:

ARCHBISHOP THOMAS ARUNDEL

Jan. 8, 1397. Isabelle, Queen Consort to Richard II (1377–99)
Oct. 13, 1399. Henry IV (1399–1413)
Feb. 26, 1403. Joan, Queen Consort to Henry IV (1399–1413)
April 9, 1413. Henry V (1413–22)

ARCHBISHOP THOMAS CARDINAL BOURCHIER

June 29, 1461. Edward IV (1461–83)
May 26, 1465. Elizabeth, Queen Consort to Edward IV (1461–83)
July 6, 1483. Richard III (1377–99)
Oct. 30, 1485. Henry VII (1485–1509)

Get My Drift, Friend William? During an audience with Charles II (1660–85), Quaker William Penn failed to remove his hat. Somewhat frustrated, Charles made such a display of removing his own hat it caused Penn to ask the King why he had done it. "Tis the custom of this house for only one person to remain covered at a time!" was the royal response.

Q Which of her two crowns does Elizabeth II take with her when she goes on foreign tours?

A Neither. Her crowns, and other items of the Crown Jewels, are not permitted out of the country. However, she does take jewelry estimated to be worth in excess of $1 million from her personal collection. Seen above, left, the St. Edward's Crown. It was copied during the reign of Charles II (1660–85) from the ancient crown worn by Edward the Confessor (1042–66) and is the Crown of England. On the right is the Imperial State Crown, which is worn by the reigning monarch on all state occasions. Made in 1838, it embodies many historical gems, including the Black Prince's ruby and a sapphire from the ring of Edward the Confessor. In the front is the 309-carat Star of Africa, cut from the Cullinan Diamond. In total this crown contains 2,783 diamonds, 277 pearls, 17 sapphires, 11 emeralds, and 5 rubies.

—British Information Services

REPRODUCTION OF THE ACTUAL INSTRUMENT OF ABDICATION

Below is a copy of the actual Instrument of Abdication executed by Edward VIII on December 10, 1936, when he gave up the throne to his brother, George VI, in order to marry "the woman I love."

INSTRUMENT OF ABDICATION

I, Edward the Eighth, of Great Britain, Ireland, and the British Dominions beyond the Seas, King, Emperor of India, do hereby declare My irrevocable determination to renounce the Throne for Myself and for My descendants, and My desire that effect should be given to this Instrument of Abdication immediately.

In token whereof I have hereunto set My hand this tenth day of December, nineteen hundred and thirty six, in the presence of the witnesses whose signatures are subscribed.

SIGNED AT
FORT BELVEDERE
IN THE PRESENCE
OF

Edward RI

Albert

Henry.

George.

ABDICATION LETTER OF EDWARD VIII
TO THE HOUSE OF COMMONS

Following is the complete text of Edward VIII's letter to the House of Commons informing them of his Abdication:

Members of the House of Commons,

After long and anxious consideration, I have determined to renounce the Throne to which I succeeded on the death of My father, and I am now communicating this, My final and irrevocable decision. Realising as I do the gravity of this step, I can only hope that I shall have the understanding of My peoples in the decision I have taken and the reasons which have led Me to take it. I will not enter now into My private feelings, but I would beg that it should be remembered that the burden which constantly rests upon the shoulders of a Sovereign is so heavy that it can only be borne in circumstances different from those in which I now find Myself. I conceive that I am not overlooking the duty that rests on Me to place in the forefront the public interest, when I declare that I am conscious that I can no longer discharge this heavy task with efficiency or with satisfaction to Myself.

I have accordingly this morning executed an Instrument of Abdication in the terms following:—(Editor's note: see facing page)

My execution of this Instrument has been witnessed by My three brothers, Their Royal Highnesses the Duke of York, the Duke of Gloucester and the Duke of Kent.

I deeply appreciate the spirit which has actuated the appeals which have been made to Me to take a different decision, and I have, before reaching My final determination, most fully pondered over them. But My mind is made up. Moreover, further delay cannot but be most injurious to the peoples whom I have tried to serve as Prince of Wales and as King and whose future happiness and prosperity are the constant wish of My heart.

I take My leave of them in the confident hope that the course which I have thought it right to follow is that which is best for the stability of the Throne and Empire and the happiness of My peoples. I am deeply sensible of the consideration which they have always extended to Me both before and after My accession to the Throne and which I know they will extend in full measure to My successor.

I am most anxious that there should be no delay of any kind in giving effect to the Instrument which I have executed and that all necessary steps should be taken immediately to secure that My lawful successor, My brother, His Royal Highness, the Duke of York, should ascend the Throne.

EDWARD R.I.

Bibliography

Listed below are fifty-nine published books from which much of the material cited in the text and captions appeared in another form or was alluded to, necessitating further research. These books represent the major works, but by no means all that were used.

Adair, John: *The Royal Palaces of Britain,* Clarkson N. Potter, New York, 1981.

Amrine, Michael, et al.: *Those Inventive Americans,* National Geographic Society, 1971.

Benson, E. F.: *King Edward VII,* Longman, London, 1933.

Bloch, Michael: *The Duke of Windsor's War,* Weidenfeld, London, 1982.

Boothroyd, Basil: *Philip: An Informal Biography,* Longman, London, 1971.

Brown, Craig, and Cunliffe, Lesley: *The Book of Royal Lists,* Routledge & Kegan Paul, London, 1982.

Bryan, J., II, and Murphy, Charles: *The Windsor Story,* Granada, London, 1979.

Burnet, Alastair: *In Person the Prince and Princess of Wales,* Summit Books, New York, 1985.

Clear, Celia: *Royal Children,* Artus/Crown Publishers, New York, 1984.

Cowles, Virginia: *Edward VII and His Circle,* Hamish Hamilton, London, 1956.

Crossman, Richard: *The Back Bench Diaries,* Hamish Hamilton, London, 1978.

De Bono, Edward: *Eureka!,* Holt, Rinehart, Winston, New York, 1974.

Donaldson, Frances: *Edward VIII,* J. B. Lippincott, Philadelphia and New York, 1975.

Fisher, Graham and Heather: *Strange & Fascinating Facts About the Royal Family,* Bell/Crown Publishers, New York, 1985.

Gore, John: *King George V,* John Murray, London, 1941.

Hall, Trevor: *Invitation to a Royal Wedding,* Greenwich House/Crown Publishers, New York, 1986.

Hamilton, Willie: *My Queen and I,* Quartet Books, London, 1975.

Heyn, Ernest V.: *Fire of Genius,* Anchor/Doubleday, New York, 1976.

Hibbert, Christopher: *The Court at St. James',* Weidenfeld, London, 1979.

Hindley, Geoffrey: *History of the Royal Family,* Gallery Books, New York, 1985.

——: *The Royal Families of Europe,* Lyric Books, London, 1979.

Holden, Anthony: *Charles, Prince of Wales,* Weidenfeld, London, 1979.

——: *Their Royal Highnesses,* Weidenfeld, London, 1981.

Howard, Philip: *The British Monarchy in the 20th Century,* Hamish Hamilton, London, 1977.

Inglis, Brian: *Abdication,* Hodder & Stoughton, London, 1966.

Jackson, Stanley: *The Savoy,* Frederick Muller, London, 1964.

Judd, Denis: *King George VI,* Michael Joseph, London, 1982.

——: *Prince Philip,* Michael Joseph, London, 1984.

Junor, Penny: *Diana, Princess of Wales,* Sidgwick & Jackson, London, 1982.

Keay, Douglas: *Royal Pursuit,* Severn House, London, 1983.

Lacey, Robert: *Majesty,* Hutchinson, London, 1977.

——: *Princess,* Hutchinson, London, 1982.

Longford, Elizabeth: *Elizabeth R.,* Weidenfeld, London, 1983.

——: *The Royal House of Windsor,* Weidenfeld, London, 1974.

——: *Victoria R.I.,* Weidenfeld, London, 1964.

Mosley, Diana: *The Duchess of Windsor,* Stein & Day, Briarcliff Manor, N.Y., 1981.

Nicolson, Harold: *King George V,* Constable, London, 1952.

——: *Monarchy,* Weidenfeld, London, 1962.

Pearson, John: *Edward the Rake,* Weidenfeld, London, 1975.

——: *The Selling of the Royal Family,* Simon & Schuster, New York, 1986.

Petrie, Charles: *Modern British Monarchy,* Eyre, London, 1961.

Philip, H.R.H. Prince: *Prince Philip Speaks,* Collins, London, 1960.

——: *Selected Speeches,* Oxford University Press, London, 1957.

Ponsonby, Frederick: *Recollections of Three Reigns,* Eyre, London, 1951.

Pope-Hennessy, James: *Queen Mary, 1867–1953,* Allen & Unwin, London, 1953.

Robertson, Patrick: *The Book of Firsts,* Bramhall/Crown, New York, 1982.

Rose, Kenneth: *George V,* Weidenfeld, London, 1983.

Sanders, Dennis: *The First of Everything,* Dell/Delacorte, New York, 1981.

Sitwell, Osbert: *Queen Mary and Others,* Michael Joseph, London, 1974.

Smith, Bernie: *The Joy of Trivia,* Bell/Crown Publishers, New York, 1976.

Sutton, Horace: *Travelers,* William Morrow, New York, 1980.

Taute, Anne: *The Kings and Queens of Great Britain* (genealogical chart), Elm Tree Books, London, 1970.

Thompson, David: *Europe Since Napoleon,* Alfred A. Knopf, New York, 1957.

Townsend, Peter: *Time and Chance,* Collins, London, 1978.

Truman, Margaret: *Harry S. Truman,* William Morrow, New York, 1973.

Wallace, Irving, and Wallechinsky, David: *The People's Almanac #3,* William Morrow, New York, 1981.

Windsor, The Duchess of: *The Heart Has Its Reasons,* Michael Joseph, London, 1956.

Windsor, H.R.H. The Duke of: *A King's Story,* Putnam, New York, 1947.

Ziegler, Philip: *Crown and Crown People,* Collins, London, 1978.

ENCYCLOPEDIA

The Encyclopaedia Britannica and its annual updates, through and including *The Book of the Year 1986,* were used for biographical information about various royals and to provide confirmation of information otherwise found in only one source.

PERIODICALS

Particular issues and page numbers would be too numerous to list individually. The sources listed below were searched for specific information, usually on and around known dates for birthdays, anniversaries, engagements, marriages, coronations, and other major events in the lives of the royals. The Abdication crisis and the World War II years, however, generated coverage over a period of years.

The Associated Press (member newspapers)
The Bayonne Times
The Jersey Journal
Life Magazine
Look Magazine
* *The Monarchy in Britain*
The New York Times
Parade
People
Time Magazine
The Times of London
United Press International (member newspapers)

---

* British Information Services publication.

Index

ABOUT THE AUTHOR

Besides *The Royal Family Quiz & Fact Book,* Timothy B. Benford is the author of four other books, three of which are also quiz and fact from Harper & Row: *The World War II Quiz & Fact Book* (1982); *The World War II Quiz & Fact Book,* Volume 2 (1984); and *The Space Program Quiz & Fact Book* (1985), co-authored with Brian Wilkes. His first novel, *Hitler's Daughter* (1983), received a Porgie Award as one of the "best paperback originals of the year" and is being made into a major feature film. A former award-winning newspaper and magazine editor, he has also won awards for magazine and newspaper freelance feature writing. He has been vice president of three of the largest public relations agencies in the country and now operates his own agency. His work has been honored with multiple awards in this field also. Tim resides with his wife, Marilyn, an award-winning travel columnist, and their two grown children, Susan and Timothy III, in Mountainside, New Jersey.